Safeguarding
Autistic Girls

of related interest

Supporting Spectacular Girls
A Practical Guide to Developing Autistic Girls' Wellbeing and Self-Esteem
Helen Clarke
ISBN 978 1 78775 548 2
eISBN 978 1 78775 549 9

A Guide to Mental Health Issues in Girls and
Young Women on the Autism Spectrum
Diagnosis, Intervention and Family Support
Dr Judy Eaton
ISBN 978 1 78592 092 9
eISBN 978 1 78450 355 0

Working with Girls and Young Women with
an Autism Spectrum Condition
A Practical Guide for Clinicians
Fiona Fisher Bullivant
ISBN 978 1 78592 420 0
eISBN 978 1 78450 784 8

Social Work with Autistic People
Essential Knowledge, Skills and the Law for Working with Children and Adults
Yo Dunn
Forewords by Alex Ruck Keene and Ruth Allen
ISBN 978 1 78592 079 0
eISBN 978 1 78450 339 0

SAFEGUARDING AUTISTIC GIRLS

Strategies for Professionals

Carly Jones MBE

Foreword by Dr Luke Beardon

Jessica Kingsley Publishers
London and Philadelphia

First published in Great Britain in 2022
by Jessica Kingsley Publishers
An Hachette Company

5

Copyright © Carly Jones MBE 2022
Foreword copyright © Dr Luke Beardon 2022

Front cover image source: Shutterstock®.

A CIP catalogue record for this title is available from the
British Library and the Library of Congress

ISBN 978 1 78775 759 2
eISBN 978 1 78775 760 8

Printed and bound in Great Britain by CPI Group (UK) Ltd, Croydon CR0 4YY

Jessica Kingsley Publishers' policy is to use papers that are natural,
renewable and recyclable products and made from wood grown in sustainable forests. The logging and manufacturing processes are expected to
conform to the environmental regulations of the country of origin.

Jessica Kingsley Publishers
Carmelite House
50 Victoria Embankment
London EC4Y 0DZ

www.jkp.com

Dedicated to all the real Autistic women and girls behind the case studies. You are all the strongest girls I will ever know. Autistic Girl Power.

Contents

Foreword

It used to be the case that the world's population could be split into two: those fortunate enough to know Carly Jones, MBE, and those unfortunates who had yet to have that absolute pleasure; I'm one of the lucky ones, by the way. Now, however, there is a third option – to get to know Carly via this fabulous narrative that is an essential read – I was going to write 'an essential read for...' and end the sentence with something along the lines of 'anyone interested in Autism, blah, blah, blah'. Sense took over, though – this book is, literally, an essential read. For everyone. If I had my way it would be statutory reading within education without exception.

Why? Because it is a life-changing book.

It might not change the lives of everyone who reads it, but the potential for it to be life-changing to many is evident as one reads through the book. Its importance cannot be underestimated.

I was worried about reading this; well – firstly, I was delighted that Carly had asked me in the first place, but the nature of the subject is not something that filled me with joy; I was anxious, to put it mildly, that I would struggle emotionally and be left feeling way worse about the world than before I started. And yet, it seems that Carly has done the nigh on impossible. She has written about horrendous situations in a way that is hard hitting (emotional roller coaster is as apt a phrase as can be in reference to reading this book) and yet alleviates the potential for negativity with such a sublime narrative style, with such gentleness and sensitivity, with such wry humour that the words never become overwhelming.

Carly has an extraordinary presence in real life – and she has managed to imbue her book with the essence of Carly in such a way that, on reading, I never felt alone; she remained a comforting companion throughout, which, I suspect, will be vital for many of the vulnerable people who are yet to read this publication.

The book itself is so full of wisdom, has so many gems of useful, pertinent suggestions and information, and covers such a vast array of beneficial areas of life that on finishing it I was drawn back to page one to read it again. Then once more to make it three. All of this was in one sitting, by the way. Carly's style is so accessible that reading is not an effort or a chore, but a delight, even taking the difficult nature of what she is writing about into account.

Don't be put off by thinking that this is all about Autistic girls/women – this book is of relevance to Autistic boys/men too. Many of the examples given could easily be understood in different contexts. It is devastating that the book is necessary, that the abuse of Autistic people is so prevalent, that Autistic people have to suffer to such a degree. Challenging preconceptions (if you don't believe Autistic folk have a sense of humour, or empathy, prepare to be challenged) in all sorts of ways, though, this book reaches beyond abuse and vulnerability, and has a positivity throughout that is heart-warming and uplifting.

Carly writes: *I don't want to use up all your time and the entire book's word count on various accounts of my life story as it feels self-indulgent. We would be here for weeks and I don't want to bore you to tears.*

My response? Bring on the next book, Carly Jones...

Dr Luke Beardon

Introduction

Hello there, welcome to the Introduction of my book, *Safeguarding Autistic Girls: Strategies for Professionals.*

I'm not going to lie to you and sell this book as one that critics would describe as "hard to put down", quite the contrary it's going to be a book that's hard to pick up. It was a hard book to write and after a year of typing away at the laptop and taking mental health breaks to process the upheaval of emotions it brought to the surface, I'll be candid with you: I never wanted to lay eyes on it again. It is with that disclaimer that I hope and thank you for finding the strength to read it, even if it is just once.

It's not going to be a lighthearted read that is bought at Heathrow for your cocktail-laden holidays (if you do just this, no judgement, I like your strategy). It's more likely to be the book that you'll reach for when someone you support has found life's rock bottom and you need jargon-free, honest, tried-and-tested strategies fast.

It's not going to be easy to digest either, as you will be (from the point this Introduction ends) walking in the shoes of some of the most heart-breaking cases, patterns of abuse and misunderstandings faced by Autistic girls, with an aim to make sure together we break the cycle.

Autistic girls are never more vulnerable than when their vulnerabilities are not known by those who care for them.

There is a risk to that too, of course. By writing a book demonstrating the loopholes found when safeguarding Autistic girls, could it be used in the wrong hands as a manual on how to exploit them? That fear is behind every word I typed. So, from this point onwards I need faith that those who are reading this are doing so with a view to make things better. I therefore ask you to please try at least one strategy to make a difference; just one pebble in the sea makes a vast wave of ripple effects in an Autistic girl's life.

I wanted to write an extensive book about safeguarding many years ago and reasoned myself out of it thanks to the fears mentioned above. So, why now?

Well, first, because the lovely Lynda and team at Jessica Kingsley Publishers emailed and asked me to write it, but logistics aside, "right now" is actually, for so many, not fast enough at all; although diagnosis of Autistic girls has thankfully skyrocketed in the last ten plus years, when it comes to their safeguarding not much is changing.

It is time to skyrocket Autistic girls' safety too.

The patterns of abuse and mistreatment of Autistic girls that we saw in the 80s and 90s are still as routine today. Day in day out, my office, emails and social media inboxes are full of requests for strategies to help yet another Autistic girl in a vulnerable situation that keeps happening to them like clockwork, day by day, month by month, year by year. It's a race against time for them all in a timeless systematic flow chart.

Autistic girls' vulnerabilities have been seen in generation after generation: the same journeys without understanding, support and strategies are mapped out, in the most heart-wrenchingly predictable pattern.

Patterns, however, are also our greatest ally. Predicting patterns with execution of strategy gives us a chance to mitigate some of the worst forms of abuse. A huge and heavy task lies ahead, then.

I'm still not really selling this book, am I? I'll try harder; in a quest to write a good enough introduction for you to feel confident to continue reading material that will likely make an empathetic professional scream into a pillow with frustration, I took it upon myself to run an internet search for "*How to write a good introduction*". The internet came up with the following suggestions:

Tell the reader what problem you aim to solve

My aim is to give insights and real-life case studies of how things can go wrong for Autistic girls, to share these insights with professionals working with Autistic girls with an aim to ensure that Autistic girls are better safeguarded, have equal chances to education, safe and happy friendships, relationships and therefore a safer and happier future.

Reveal the strategies (but not all of them)

I will offer strategies that are low cost. You will learn how Autistic girls struggle to recognize and report abuse, why this happens and how just one simple question, "What was the best thing and what was the worst thing that happened to you today?", asked each day, can help safeguard them.

Prove to the reader why you are the expert they should listen to; build your credibility

I have a particular loathing for anyone who describes themselves as an expert. If other people call someone an expert that's kind and often true, but to sell yourself as an expert is a bit like those blokes who introduce themselves as the most attractive man in the room at a party. It is not only grossly narcissistic, it's also subjective to the person looking at you. What lies beneath the veneer depends on who else is in the room and, anyway, it is ultimately an accolade that only lasts so long.

Advocacy is the same. You may be in a room where you are the most experienced in that subject matter. Change the subject matter or change the room and the expert label is gone. I do not like to advertise myself as an expert, or an academic. I am Autistic, diagnosed at 32 after a life of vast vulnerability, near misses, misunderstandings and upheaval. I left school at 15 with no GCSEs, pregnant, and ended up living in a mother and baby hostel. My qualifications gained whilst living in that hostel were A level equivalents from an apprentice in a legal office (see Employment in Chapter 5) and Open University social sciences in my early 20s. I don't have a degree though. I failed it. I ran out of money when I got divorced at 25.

My creditability is solely that of duty and dedication, albeit not to a doctorate. I know what I know from experience and I am happy to share that alongside my professional advocacy insights and years of loophole-spotting experience. It is not going to be everyone's cup of tea, but if it helps one person who then helps another, and another, it will be worth it anyway.

How will this book work?

I have written words and you will, I hope, read some words.

Make the reader a promise

That's a big commitment! I am not fond of making promises I can't keep. The promise I *can* keep is that by writing about Autistic girls I in no way solely want to safeguard girls. When writing this book, almost every time I typed "Autistic girls" I yearned to type "and boys!" straight after. There is a genuine reason the book is focused on girls and I hope to do justice to the explanation for that when I discuss intersectionality in Chapter 4. I promise also that every case story you hear is true and has happened: be it recent, a few years ago or over 20 or 30 years ago. I have, of course, changed the names and in some cases the ages of those in the case studies. This is to provide the real girls and their loved ones behind the case studies protection, anonymity and the chance to have a future without their darkest times being aired. I have a confession too: some, but not all, of these case studies are actually my own younger life experiences and learning curves with age and name changed. I have been told this is something many professionals who cannot disclose the fact they are Autistic do frequently in their writings. I, of course, am out loud and proud about being Autistic and I have no fear in writing about my past. It is not just about me though, is it? As a parent, daughter, cousin and sister, I also have a duty to safeguard my own family's feelings and right to privacy – hence the name changes. Some case studies are a roundup of an almost identical situation that has been faced by hundreds of girls and women I have worked with over the years. In fact, I cannot think of one case study that has only happened to one Autistic girl. Had it been an isolated event I probably would not have mentioned it in the book as it's the patterns we are looking for. The promise, however, is the same – all case studies are, sadly, true. Despite that, I promise to try to make you laugh. It seems a thoroughly inappropriate promise to make in such a serious subject matter, but humour, normally self-deprecating, has in the past seemed to help in keynotes and lectures as a palette cleanser between servings of heavy and hard to swallow courses.

Make a call to action

Grab tea, wine if it helps. Deep breath, and I offer you a virtual hand hold here: let's start.

CHAPTER I

The Current Situation

Why are Autistic girls vulnerable?

Autistic girls' biggest vulnerability is that they are often hidden in plain sight. If we don't know that an Autistic girl is Autistic to start with, we cannot support her to become less vulnerable. And even if she does have a known diagnosis of Autism, if we do not know the specific risks that Autistic girls face, how can we mitigate against those risks?

For example, many Autistic people experience prosopagnosia, often spoken about in layman's terms as face blindness; it means having difficulty recognizing people's faces well. Many Autistic people with prosopagnosia are not able to immediately recognize their friends, family members, teachers etc., especially out of context, seeing them in a place where they would not expect to see them. (You may find friends of Autistic girls have a very distinctive accent, hair style or colour and style of dressing; it's possible that the Autistic girl feels more comfortable with them as they recognize them better. I don't think this is often a conscious choice but as humans we tend to be drawn to those we feel comfortable with and are happy to see, so naturally recognizing someone is a good start!)

Face blindness can leave Autistic girls even more vulnerable to getting into trust-based situations with people they don't really know as they may assume it is someone else. Imagine the impact for an Autistic girl when she struggles to recognize faces and a stranger approaches her in the street convincing her they know her from a youth club or recent party, but they are lying? Imagine how vulnerable an Autistic girl who experiences face blindness is outside the school gate to being picked up by someone posing as her mum's friend. It doesn't bear thinking about, but we must, as we are here to safeguard. But if you were not aware that many Autistic girls struggle to recognize faces out of context, how would you know that you need to find ways to safeguard her both from stranger danger and from people she's been told to be wary around?

If you weren't aware that some Autistic girls do not know when they are in pain, or hungry or thirsty would you develop routines to ensure she is healthy and serious illnesses are treated in a timely way, potentially saving her life? There is much more on this in Chapter 5.

Autistic girls all too often get left behind. The reasons for this are wide and varied. In 2015 I undertook an informal survey to explore this in more detail (this is a method I use a lot to ensure I'm not just basing my thinking on my own perspective).[1] This research showed that 91 per cent of Autistic adults had experienced some form of abuse before their Autism diagnosis. The same informal survey research, however, also showed that after diagnosis, support and building self-awareness, up to 73 per cent of Autistic adults questioned have been safer, either as they had not experienced abuse or had the self-awareness to spot abuse, prevent it or report it in a timely fashion.

Autistic girls growing up are likely to have difficulty navigating the social aspect of boundaries, as very often they are already out of their comfort zone when with friends and peers. This can often mean they go into "remote control" mode and passively follow the group in order to manage and keep up.

As you may be aware, many Autistic girls struggle with social imagination. In short, this can mean foreseeing what is consequential in social contexts; in slightly longer form it can mean being able to look at social situations and interpret what could happen for each of the people involved in a social situation. A social situation, of course, is not always a big event, social gathering or a party. A phone call, group text message and a table of friends and peers at university or school is a social situation.

Social imagination differences could look like a 15-year-old Autistic girl being very honest and unfiltered about who her crush is with the other girls on her table in maths who may immediately report back to her crush's girlfriend later that day, causing the Autistic girl great embarrassment and to likely to be in trouble. She didn't predict that this would be the consequence. It could look like a 13-year-old Autistic girl who reads a text message and does not reply as she didn't realize the other person needed confirmation before they planned to meet later in the day. It could be the 22-year-old Autistic woman who struggles with managing her budget because she is paid on the 27th of the month and sees enough money in her bank to afford the new laptop she needs but didn't think forward to how much money would be left to pay the bills/friends she owes money to on the 1st of the month. In more serious cases, it could be the 17-year-old Autistic girl who didn't foresee the consequences that, by continuing an unplanned pregnancy, she would be working two jobs and doing the school run five years from now and still not going to her university of choice hundreds of miles away from home. It is therefore important for those of us involved in safeguarding to read up on social imagination and develop a strategy to help girls attempt to navigate this, and to give them safer independence when they are older.

It is important professionals know Autistic girls' differences in order to have the tools to understand and safeguard them as much as they can. There are more hurdles in doing so I am afraid, but it's better to be honest in discussing these differences in order to manage them and make life less dangerous in the long term.

If Autistic girls were not already made more vulnerable by

their social imagination differences, they are also facing the hurdle of what some academics refer to as the "theory of mind". It's suggested that the theory of mind is the ability to know that another person's brain may have different thoughts, feelings, wants and agendas to your own.

The "Double Empathy Problem", or DEP, amplified by the work of Dr Damian Milton who has undertaken research into the Double Empathy Problem, demonstrates that issues in communication between Autistic and non-Autistic individuals are not the fault of Autistic people alone, but rather are a breakdown of mutual understanding between humans who experience and view the world differently. As stated in the Introduction, this isn't an academic book, it's a practical safeguarding book, so if academia is your bag, please do read the brilliant work of Dr Milton to get more insight. It is in short layman's terms that I proceed.

If it is the case that Autistic people (and their non-Autistic family and friends) struggle with this mutual understanding, it would be easy for the Autistic young person to assume a lot of things:

- An Autistic young person may assume someone loves them deeply...as they love that person deeply.

- They may assume that someone is loyal to them...as they are loyal to them.

- They may assume someone really means what they say...as they really mean what they say to them.

- They may assume that someone will not do anything to hurt them...as they would not do anything to hurt them.

- They may assume that if they are hurt or abused that their trusted adult knows it happened...as they are fully aware it happened.

It is very easy to forget to share information with someone when you assume they already know that information, because you know it yourself.

I can recall well a professional once asking me how on earth I could be Autistic and enjoy acting. His perception was that an Autistic female could not possibly act as it would require "putting myself in someone else's shoes". My reply was: "I don't do that, but I've learned how to allow a character to walk in my shoes instead."

STRATEGIES AND TIPS

This section will focus on practical steps we can take when we're aware of some of the challenges Autistic girls may be facing.

We can support Autistic girls who have face blindness from a young age. If it's her birthday party and friends will be arriving – not in school where she knows them and not in uniform how she normally sees them – suggest to her parents they provide name labels for her guests. They don't have to say why (as this might embarrass her) they could just say it's needed for the entertainer or to hand out the right party bag. Be inventive!

As an Autistic girl gets older her face blindness can be supported by friends, teachers, colleagues and support workers but these must of course be trusted adults and friends. If you are working in an office or conference environment do make sure that your name badge is clearly worn. This helps Autistic women tremendously in the workplace. If there is a team meeting or new employee starting, make sure an email with photos and a short biography is sent to all staff in advance.

There is no research about this yet that I know of (anyone reading looking to do a PhD please consider this!), but I know from first-hand experience Autism assistance dogs can provide excellent "friend" and "foe" alarms for Autistic girls.

Arranging for an assistance dog may be worth exploring with the girls or families you support. As well as potentially helping with safeguarding, they can provide sensory comfort and companionship too.

If Autistic girls have an issue understanding that people can have an agenda/plan/want/like that differs to their own, are we then also able to assume that if we do not really like someone, they do not like us? Discuss this idea with the Autistic girl you support. Could there be people who really, genuinely like her that she is unaware of? Also discuss with non-Autistic girls how to extend the offer of friendship in a clear and explicit way to Autistic girls they want to be friends with.

We need to spot these breakdowns in communication in everyday life as well as when it has created issues that are being handled by professionals.

Perhaps the Autistic girl you are supporting often assumes she answered a text/email as in her mind she had replied to the question, when in reality she hasn't responded. Perhaps the other person didn't make their text or email clear that it required a reply, so the Autistic girl didn't see the urgency to reply at all, with potential consequences for making and maintaining that friendship.

She may assume that as she dislikes an activity/food/ TV show so does another person. The other person may not understand that the Autistic girl could find certain activities, foods, shows overwhelming. Encourage the Autistic girl you support to think through what another person knows/ what that might mean for her own actions, and encourage non-Autistic friends to be patient and explicit about their needs/expectations.

Can you recall a time when there was a breakdown in communication in the past? If you can, it's probably a good indicator that the Autistic girl you support struggles with communicating her knowledge to make it shared knowledge, and that the non-Autistic people in her life are struggling to communicate their knowledge to share it with the Autistic girl.

On an upbeat note, if the Autistic girls you support tend to assume that others have the same information in their brains as they do, do they really appreciate how many things they can do, their talents and wisdom and how many things they know that others do not?

They may have often assumed that people have the same intellect and skills as they do, when maybe others do not. It is worth mentioning this to the Autistic girl you support. When someone was kind enough to tell me this it really helped me to not quit on projects that I had worked hard on but assumed wouldn't help anyone (this book being one of them!).

If the Autistic girl you support struggles to understand her talents, value and intelligence this could well be why. It is important their support team helps them recognize their strengths as well as their challenges.

Professionals who work with Autistic girls would do well to try to understand how difficult it is to comprehend consequences (social imagination) when they only have their own knowledge or own feedback to rely on.

I have found a way to attempt to communicate to non-Autistic professionals how having only our own insights and feedback to rely on feels. It is a tad unorthodox but has had some success in the past. It involves a traditional game of "consequences"; my late Nan used to play this with me on Boxing Day as a kid somewhere in the 80s.

You'll need a colleague (this is important; the admin work can wait!) one sheet of paper and a pen. I will wait until you get back...

Back? Great, let's get cracking.

1. You and your colleague take turns in contributing

parts of a story. You MUST hide what you have written by folding the paper before handing it back to your partner.

   a. Colleague – choose a name (write boy's name)

   b. You – say who they met (write girl's name)

   c. Colleague – in/at/on… (write where they met)

   d. You – he said (write what he said)

   e. Colleague – she said (write what she said)

   f. You – his action (write what he did)

   g. Colleague – her action (write what she did)

   h. You – the consequence was (write what happened).

2. When all stages of the writing game are done, you can unfold the fan and the final story is read out, usually with unexpected and awkward results.

Foreseeing the consequence was difficult, wasn't it?

Now imagine you are a 14-year-old Autistic girl and it's a text conversation with a friend.

Now imagine you are an Autistic girl and it's a WhatsApp group chat of five girls from school.

Now imagine it's a classroom of 30.

Now imagine it's someone who doesn't have your best intentions at heart.

Now imagine this every day for every conversation from the day you were born for the rest of your life.

You get the idea.

That may be why although some of the subjects we will discuss in this book could, mostly, affect any teen girl, the vulnerability of an Autistic girl is often extreme with a different cause, a different perspective, and a different impact. It therefore requires a different solution and different strategies. The ability to talk in no way means the ability to report abuse in a timely fashion.

Team diagnosed vs. team undiagnosed

The memories of the challenges and vulnerability I faced at 14 without anyone who understood Autistic girls to support me, and recalling the desire I felt for someone who knew how to grab me out of that particular fire, has naturally turned me into an adult who tries to save other young girls from an inferno of life events that I know I can help them extinguish.

My diagnosis came late, at 32. The day after I was diagnosed, I sent a bunch of flowers to my doctor, Dr. Judith Gould, and the Lorna Wing Centre team saying "Thank you for the first day of the rest of my life."

Why? Because it truly was. Diagnosis day was the day I understood a voluminous catalogue of vulnerabilities, mistakes, and experiences for which I had, until that day, blamed myself for entirely. Diagnosis gave me not an excuse but a reason – a salvation – and the fresh start that I desperately needed at 14, not 32. Better late than never.

So, although I've been working in Autism awareness and advocacy since 2008 with my "mum hat" – advocating for Autistic women and girls as a mum of two Austistic daughters (diagnosed at six and two years old) – July 2nd, 2014 was when my authentically Autistic life started following my own astronomically late diagnosis at 32.

My work for younger Autistic females who are yet to be diagnosed is fuelled by this great privilege of an official diagnosis, the hindsight that gives me the knowledge and hope that their lives too can be changed for the better.

Often, I've heard Autistic adults on social media lightheartedly say they are only "4, 8 or 10 in Autistic years", nodding to the length of time since they were diagnosed. I want to make sure the next generation don't have to wait 32 years. I don't want those who self-identify as Autistic but can't access an official diagnosis to have to wait in what feels like no (wo)man's land. Not quite "normal" enough to flourish happily in their lives, but not quite "disabled" enough to access the peer groups, support and understanding they need. (Note: using the word normal here didn't feel right – what is normal anyway? I just couldn't think of a clearer way to describe it.)

Why does a diagnosis matter?

Every teen Autistic girl will have her own reasons for wanting a diagnosis (or not). But younger girls whose parents are leading the path to diagnosis often ask me WHY a diagnosis matters. Some of my responses and thoughts on why diagnosis is important are listed below.

As professionals in whatever capacity, we need to safeguard. Diagnosis is the first step towards that.

Sometimes parents who are very wealthy feel there isn't any issue that their Autistic daughter will face that money cannot smooth out. To a point they are right; wealthy families can afford a private diagnosis, which they can then decide to share with their daughter's NHS GP or not. Wealthy families won't have to rely on carer and DLA payments in order to financially cover the (often extensive) extra costs of raising an Autistic daughter; they can afford for one parent to not work and offer 24/7 care and supervision, can afford for private tutors to visit the home where their daughter feels comfortable rather than sending her to a school she can't cope in, or can pick and choose a small private school and a class with a handful of children.

This isn't to say that wealthy parents of Autistic girls have an easier time of it. Autistic young people often have Autistic parents, often undiagnosed due to the better understanding of Autism emerging only in more recent decades. In my years of advocacy I've seen many parents of Autistic girls, some of whom are also Autistic themselves, being conned out of their hard-earned cash, paying out tens of thousands of pounds in "treatments" for their daughters' "mental health issues"; being misled ethically, medically and educationally, with private school off-rolling (to put it bluntly, getting rid of) their Autistic daughter yet holding vast fees back, often given the loophole to do so as the private schools in question are not monitored or accountable to the same standards state schools are. In some cases, being wealthy has exposed parents to con artists selling them therapies or treatments that won't work and do cause distress to their daughters.

There are some issues that a diagnosis helps with, regardless of money, and these include access to support from the medical and legal professions. Later in the book I will delve much deeper into why it is vital a doctor or health care professional knows their patient is Autistic. For now, let's just note that a diagnosis can help to safeguard an Autistic girl's access to healthcare.

Similarly: legal issues. At some point in life, people are likely to face legal issues, perhaps a court case as a defendant, a victim or a witness. If the authorities are not aware their defendant, victim or witness is Autistic there is every chance that, through nobody's fault, they won't be treated fairly, for example because they may not be questioned in an appropriate way – again, more on this later in the book.

Thinking more broadly about the importance of diagnosis, how about the Autistic girl's sense of self? Her identity? Without a sense of self, she cannot create a self-identity. Without self-identity she will struggle to grow self-confidence. No self-confidence leads to struggling to value herself, her boundaries and her happiness. These are all important ingredients in the plight to safeguard.

An Autistic girl prior to diagnosis WILL know she is different; she will know she is struggling in friendships, saying what is constantly perceived as the wrong thing, experiencing the world's sights, tastes, smells and sounds more intensely than others. She will know she isn't keeping up or fitting in. A diagnosis gives the foundation from which to begin to find the answers to her questions. It stops her blaming herself and, instead of feeing like a walking deficit, she may start to feel like she has a wonderful difference.

An Autism diagnosis can help mitigate misdiagnosis of other conditions too. Autism is not a mental health issue. Autistic people can also have mental health issues, just as anyone can, but being Autistic and undiagnosed often results in an Autistic girl's natural Autistic traits (such as behaviour in a large group) being misunderstood. This leaves Autistic girls very vulnerable to having a misdiagnosis and medication for a mental health condition they simply don't have.

It takes a village to raise a child, for an Autistic girl we need to construct a village of multidisciplinary professionals working with and not against her or her parents. On top of this, wider family understanding is needed; a diagnosis can stop the "isn't she just lazy/naughty/rebellious/rude/aloof" remarks from perhaps older or extended family members, and instead give family members the chance to read up on Autistic girls, share that information with others and together learn how to better support the Autistic girl at the heart of their care. Maybe that is why you are reading this book now (thanks by the way!). Knowing what Autism is, what it can mean and what vulnerabilities it may incur enables us to really start to support in a meaningful way.

If we don't know what Autistic girls' vulnerabilities are, how can we support them to become less vulnerable?

If I tell you that the life expectancy of Autistic people with an additional learning disability is 39.5 years of age and the life expectancy of Autistic people without an additional learning disability is 58 years,[2] does it reinforce how important their diagnosis is? Does it make you appreciate their desire to learn, create, master, achieve, invent, love, decode, nurture, campaign, and care for animals? Their abrupt honesty and unfiltered communication as they leave no words unsaid, dance and sing like no one is watching, at times leaves you to wonder if they have no embarrassment gene; they seem to embrace each day as if their time here may well be shorter and somehow they know it.

So, why the wait?

I believe a diagnosis is a human right; currently a diagnosis is a privilege. Sadly, it's not as easy as noticing a girl is Autistic and making an appointment and getting an official diagnosis. There are many, many gates and many gatekeepers in this process of waiting for a diagnosis that is often referred to as the diagnosis pathway.

Perhaps it is more like trying to find the answer in an *Alice in Wonderland*-style door-opening task or taking a hike up Everest than a whimsical pathway stroll in the New Forest, but a pathway it is nonetheless. So, what are these gates and who are the gatekeepers? Brace yourself as we look a little closer at the process.

Gate 1: The postcode lottery

The UK's local authorities and regions have various waiting list times.[3] The national average is approximately two years for an Autism diagnosis. At the time of writing Berkshire, where I live, has the longest waiting time in the country. I do not see this as a poor reflection on the local services though – quite the contrary. Often a long waiting list, although frustrating for professionals and parents alike, can be an indicator of good models of practice of diagnosis. After all you wouldn't queue up for years hoping for a reservation at a fast food chain, but you may well do so for a once in a lifetime Michelin star restaurant booking. An area with a long waiting list can be a positive indicator of the level of awareness about Autism and girls in that area and the lack of stigma about being Autistic. Waiting for diagnosis is, of course, frustrating; and waiting can carry risks to health and even life.

Gate 2: Different diagnostic tools

There are a number of diagnostic tools used to diagnose Autism.[4] As not all clinicians who diagnose Autism are required to have trained in all the various diagnostic tools, the area you live in will impact on which diagnostic tool is used (and thus affect the likelihood of receiving a diagnosis). Simply, clinicians in your area may have the clinical experience of Autistic girls to assess their Autistic traits and confidently diagnose them, or they may not.

Although at all times I try to remain balanced, my personal and professional opinion is that all clinicians who diagnose Autism in the UK should be duty-bound to have trained in using the DISCO tool. Why? Well, partly because I was diagnosed under the DISCO myself, but mostly because, in my professional experience, it is an effective diagnostic tool for use with the most vulnerable and hard-to-reach Autistic girls, some of whom might no longer be with us without diagnosis, but who can live well and thrive with a diagnosis that opens the door to support and self-acceptance. If this were a research paper or a history book my view here could be seen as biased; to a degree, it may well be. Luckily, this is a non-academic book about safeguarding!

The DISCO, despite its name, is not a party in a posh frock. It's actually The Diagnostic Interview for Social and Communication Disorders. This is a semi-structured interview designed to find out about the person's development, behaviour and skills since birth through to their current day-to-day experiences.

The DISCO was developed for use at the Lorna Wing Centres, by the late Dr Lorna Wing OBE and Dr Judith Gould, for use with children, young people and adults of any age. Its beauty is that the DISCO collects information using a dimensional approach and concerning all aspects of each individual's skills and challenges. The DISCO can be used with children, young people and adults of any age, for any level of ability, for Autistic people who may be clearly Autistic to the clinician, and those whom many clinicians could risk overlooking as they haven't looked deeply enough to see that person's Autistic life experiences. The DISCO can also assist in identifying other conditions which Autistic people sometimes have as well as being Autistic, such as ADHD, tics, dyspraxia and catatonia. So, you get a profile report of what your needs are as well as your strengths.

ADOS (Autism Diagnostic Observation Schedule) is an alternative to the DISCO. The ADOS is a semi-structured, standardized assessment of communication, social interaction, and play or imaginative use of materials for individuals who have been referred for investigation.

Some of my family members were diagnosed under the ADOS. I find it a good tool for diagnosis of Autistic girls *if* the clinician has great experience with diagnosing Autistic girls, or the Autistic girl's presentation in a clinical setting is very apparent.

It's a commonly used diagnostic tool and, although there seems to be an emphasis on "imaginative play" by the clinicians and professionals who use ADOS, when the clinicians are experienced in understanding the difference between play in which special interests, topics and maybe copied phrases from television shows or online videos are used *and* when the difference between traditional imagination and social imagination is understood in practice, ADOS can lead to a timely diagnosis for an Autistic girl. For example, some Autistic girls will play in a seemingly typical way in an ADOS assessment; however, with a closer eye, perhaps over a longer period, they may lead the game back to a special interest. An example of this could be a girl who adores Dr Who and only wants to talk about Dr Who. In the assessment room she was given a Barbie doll, a pair of plastic scissors and some farm animals. She lined the farm animals up as guests, and pretended to cut the Barbie's hair. When asked what the game was she said, "A wedding, dolly is getting ready for a wedding", which, left there, could have looked fairly typical. Luckily, the doctor asked, "Who is dolly getting married to?" and the young girl then replied "Dr Who!" and reeled off a list of all of Dr Who's previous companions. This is a blend of imaginative play and rigid interests.

The ADI-R is a revised version of the original ADI and the information obtained can be used in a diagnostic algorithm for Autism as described in the main international diagnostic manuals, ICD-10[5] and DSM-5.[6] The NAS website has more information.[7]

In sum, different tools can impact on rates of diagnosis, and this can have particular consequences for Autistic girls.

Gate 3: Stereotypes of Autism

In the media and on the news, Autism is often spoken about in limited ways.

In the news:

1. someone is about to get a Nobel peace prize

or:

2. someone is about to be on trial for a mass shooting.

In the media our Autistic girls' chances of representation are slightly more realistic thanks to the efforts of many producers to have Autistic girls play Autistic characters, but outside that remit it's often the case that when the character of an Autistic young person is portrayed they are male and like trains and maths, or are an adult man who's good at gambling (if only!). All of this means certain perceptions of what it is to be Autistic can be prevalent in society, and Autistic girls who do not fit that mould have an extra barrier to cross.

Gate 4: Masking and eye contact

Masking, often known as camouflaging, is where Autistic girls observe people, mimic them, practise to fit in and so suppress their authentic Autistic self in order to appear less Autistic. Masking isn't just for girls, Autistic boys mask too but Autistic girls' masking has been considered a factor in why Autistic girls go undiagnosed and why they have flown under the radar of professionals for many decades.

I once watched a wildlife documentary in which the narrator said, "The chameleon doesn't change its appearance to harm, mislead or hurt others in the environment, it simply does so to survive." The life of the chameleon resonated with me on a level I'm sure is rather unhealthy for a fully grown woman.

Elizabeth, a brilliantly intelligent 17-year-old Autistic girl, came into my office one afternoon after college and was sad as she couldn't fit in. She loved animals and (against my office rental conditions) I had sneaked my ginger tom cat, Chester, under my jumper and past security so she had something to look forward to when she arrived. Stroking Chester, she described all the ways she was trying to be like the other girls at college and how exhausted she was by it all.

"Have you heard of masking?" I said. I then told her about the chameleon documentary.

Elizabeth went quiet for a long time, I assumed she thought I was a crazy cat lady by now. "Don't be ridiculous, Carly, I'm nothing like a chameleon!"

I apologized.

She smiled: "I'm an octopus. Octopi change their colours too. The difference is they have a huge brain and three hearts!"

It's a line that I'll never forget and was definitely worth sneaking the cat in to hear (if my office team are reading this: sorry).

Many Autistic girls when masking will suss out that not making eye contact is seen as rude and makes them stand out as being different. As a child I would remove my glasses – I have extremely poor eyesight and when I took my glasses off the world became a beautiful, serene cloud of non-eyes. Hence why I've never had laser eye surgery to correct it. As an Autistic woman, I found that eye contact from others soon stopped after having double F breast implants (less invasive options to avoid eye contact are available, however!).

Other Autistic girls develop their own strategies to avoid eye contact. It could be blinking a lot, wearing sunglasses or hoodies or hats, looking away or looking behind them regularly in long conversations, or lying their head on their school desk rather than sitting up straight. It could be staring in a bid for the other party to look away. In a diagnosis room these strategies should also be viewed as "lack of eye contact".

Gate 5: Being a hyper-empath rather than having a lack of empathy

I've worked in Autism for over 13 years and 99 per cent of the Autistic girls (and boys!) I have come across have been hyper-empathetic people who have a great empathy for others' plights, the fixers of the world. Stereotypes of Autism, be that in clinical practice or in the media, may lead us to imagine an eight-year-old boy who likes fixing train-sets or takes apart a remote control to fix it. But I see Autistic girls fixing problems every day: problems which often aren't their own, problems of others which require hyper-empathy. I see Autistic girls who train and care for animals, Autistic girls who grow up to be-come engineers, cyber experts, foster parents, fabulous mums, psychologists, nurses, campaigners, volunteers at homeless shelters, surgeons, GPs, scientists, researchers, dentists, primary school teachers – all roles that require much selfless empathy.

In 2014, I helped out at Cambridge University on their ad-visory board for 'Autistic Motherhood' research with Autism Women Matter. Their researchers and wider teams are, from my first-hand experience, keen and proactive in ensuring that

Autistic girls who later become mothers are not viewed as being without empathy and are given support and understanding in family law and social services intervention.

The Empathy Quotient (EQ) is a 60-item questionnaire designed to measure empathy. The test was developed by the University of Cambridge.[8] The EQ as a tool isn't in itself the concern here, the wider concern for our younger girls is that should their particular clinician not be as clinically experienced in working with Autistic girls (the postcode lottery mentioned previously!), they may be offered a diagnostic assessment that, to put it bluntly, works against them gaining a diagnosis.

In clinical use the empathy measurements provided by the EQ can be used by mental health professionals when assessing the level of social differences in Autistic people. It's important to remember the EQ is used for adults, so Autistic girls under 18 would very likely not be EQ tested. It is often used alongside the Autism Quotient. The Autism-Spectrum Quotient Test (abbreviated to AQ) is a diagnostic questionnaire designed to measure the expression of Autism-Spectrum traits in an individual, by his or her own subjective self-assessment.[9]

It's important to remember that the AQ, like the EQ, is used for adults, not children, and is used as a self-assessment tool. It's highly unlikely an Autistic girl under 18 would be offered self-assessment of this style. So why mention it?

The issue I've seen time and time again over the last 13 years is that clinicians who diagnose under 18s also diagnose adults in the same working week; their clinical experience and use of AQ or EQ may, and in those professionals with less clinical experience of diagnosing Autistic girls often does, cloud their confidence in making an Autism diagnosis for the young girl, her family and the professionals supporting her. This leaves the Autistic girl back at square one after two years of waiting and a list of distressing undiagnosed and unsupported experiences growing by the day, but why?

Below are some examples of AQ questions (in the form of

statements which the respondent needs to agree or disagree with):

"I am fascinated by dates."

Context is needed to respond to this statement. Is this a date as in January 2nd 1987, or dates as in a bag of fish and chips down the beach with your crush? Or perhaps those squishy dried fruits your Nan gets in at Christmas?

"I find making up stories easy."

Many Autistic girls are fabulous authors and poets, they'd likely reply yes to this one, but what about the other context of stories? Does this mean lying? Making up tales about someone? That would likely get a no.

"I don't particularly enjoy reading fiction."

This will probably be expected to be agreed with, I don't know why though, as I have yet to come across any Autistic girl who doesn't have a copy of *Harry Potter*, Japanese cartoons or the like in her bag at youth club. Seems a rite of passage in fact.

"I am good at social chit chat."

I'm assuming the expectation is that this would be answered no, but Autistic girls who mask get good at social interaction. They become BAFTA/Golden Globe award-winning social butterflies. There's a wider context behind this statement that isn't asked about though. What did you have to do to PREPARE to be good at chit chat? What effect does having to be good at chit chat have on your mental health? Are you comfortable with what you overshare when you are being good at chit chat? Does being good at social chit chat make you vulnerable in social situations? That's the real question.

"I make friends easily."

Define friends: people at college, work, school, in real life?

Facebook friends or Instagram followers? An alternative question could be: "The last time you were unwell who visited you?" or: "Are you able to maintain long-term friendships?"

Similarly, if a clinician whom the Autistic girl has an appointment with hasn't diagnosed many Autistic teen girls but has a great grasp of using AQ and EQ for their adult appointments, their judgement on the Autistic girls' traits could be clouded by these EQ questions:

"I try to keep up with the current trends and fashions."
    If an Autistic girl is masking and copying her peers to blend in, she will care very much about the latest trends.

"I try to solve my own problems rather than discuss them with others."
    Not a sign of lack of empathy here. It could be a sign that the Autistic girl doesn't know how to ask for help in a timely fashion, or that she has difficulties with social imagination and understanding that advantageous consequences can occur from asking others for help.

Gate 6: Diagnostic overshadowing

In recent years, working on Boards that are rich in diverse disabled members and Chairs, I have been fortunate enough to meet some individuals who are blind, or deaf, or wheelchair users. Many have confided in me they are also Autistic, but their primary disability has meant their Autistic traits were overshadowed by their other conditions and therefore they either received their diagnosis as an adult, or not at all. I worry about the healthcare and legal implications of diagnosis overshadowing. If, for example, you are an Autistic woman undiagnosed and also using a wheelchair, will you be given physical accessibility in a court setting but not neurodivergent accessibility? If you are an Autistic woman (undiagnosed) and also blind would your sensory issues around pain and sound be considered in childbirth? Or assumed to be due to the fact you are blind?

Gate 7: Race and cultural beliefs of the family and the professionals

Autism has for far too long been seen as a "male and pale" condition. Autism is a part of human neurodiversity and is of course prevalent in all humans regardless of skin colour, geographical setting, place of birth and religion. Cultural and religious environments have led to Autism being viewed differently however. Clinicians who diagnose Autism also have their own diverse backgrounds that could affect who they diagnose and who they don't – and why. I'll expand on this in the section on intersectionality in Chapter 4.

Gate 8: They are in care, fostered or adopted

The painful Catch-22 as an advocate for safeguarding and Autistic girls is that it's often the most vulnerable girls who struggle to gain their diagnosis. Often their Autistic traits are explained away by the fact they have been abused, neglected or have had trauma in their early lives. I have seen time and time again Autistic girls in care or who have been removed from their birth family have a hugely difficult time being officially diagnosed in a timely way.

Gate 9: Socio-economic status

If your local area cannot provide a clinician trained in the diagnostic tools that understand Autistic girls' traits and their presentation of Autism, securing a private diagnosis will cost money. The socio-economic background of the Autistic girl will impact her chances of having a fair shot at a diagnosis.

STRATEGIES AND TIPS

- At all times remember that not all Autistic girls will have a diagnosis. Diagnosis is a privilege. I am no more Autistic now at 38 than I was when I was 14 in 1996. The only difference is people understand me now.

- The Equality Act is needs-led, not led by medical notes. If the Autistic girl you support has needs, her diagnosis report comes second to that, ethically and legally. There is no legal need for the Autistic girl to have a medically diagnosed condition for her to have rights. The effect on her daily life is what matters.

- I have known cases where a GP can request special funding for a private diagnosis if it is needed for an Autistic girl – this is worth looking into.

- The DISCO diagnosis tool should be part of mandatory training for all who diagnose Autism.

- Autistic girls get so good at masking they will often mask in a clinical or appointment setting. Professionals may not see what they perceive as an Autistic person at all in that appointment time or even in a whole school day. You need to see past the mask, and assess reports from all aspects of the girl's life.

- If you need to create a safe space for an Autistic girl to open up, I can highly recommend cats.

The Autistic lens vs. the mental health lens

As an Autism advocate, I know very little about mental health conditions. Autism is not a mental health condition, it is a neurological difference. It is of course possible for Autistic people to have mental health conditions as well as Autism. A mental health professional once advised me that "Autism likes to bring a friend", which I thought was a good way to explain it. Autistic girls can be solely Autistic or can be Autistic and have an additional mental health condition. Too often though, Autistic girls are misdiagnosed as having a mental health condition before their Autism diagnosis.

Karina was late for her appointment and crying with exhaustion and fear of being late when I spotted her across the building, I left my office to greet her and asked if she needed a hug. She did. Karina was heavily pregnant with twins and being misunderstood by her mental health team regarding whether she would be a fit parent. She was anxious, isolated and now late for the appointment she had obviously mustered up the last remaining brave face she had to attend. In these cases, instead of sticking strictly to the hour, I'll throw the appointment book out of the window. I didn't have another guest booked in for a few hours anyway, and there were chocolate biscuits that needed eating and a pot of tea to drink.

Karina was excited about motherhood, even though she didn't have that long to prepare for the arrivals as she didn't know she was pregnant until very recently, despite being so far gone. Her yet-to-be-born babies had already been placed in a children in need category by her local social services due to her history of mental health issues.

Karina tried to explain to me how many of her Autistic traits were considered mental health issues rather than Autism. Karina, like many Autistic girls, was misdiagnosed/diagnosed with an unstable mood disorder. For those who may not be aware of emotional processing delay in Autistic girls, it is where an event occurs, but we don't process and/or display our emotional reaction to that event, be it happy or sad, at the time, instead we do so sometime after.

Karina would have days where she was incredibly sad, and

nobody understood why as at the time she was sad there were very happy things going on for her. So why was she so distressed? What we found out, when we delved into this in our sessions together, was that she was experiencing the emotional effects of events perhaps six months later than when they happened.

Similarly, I know Autistic girls who have been misdiagnosed as being Bipolar when they are elated and happy about a wonderful event maybe six, ten, or twelve months later. Equally, when there may be upsetting events taking place, they are in an elevated mood. It can leave Autistic girls really misunderstood. In Karina's case it was highly likely one of the factors that led to her newborns being removed from her care.

I could relate in some small part to Karina's experiences of her mood being misinterpreted. I struggle with this too.

Several years ago, I lost a loved one quite suddenly. A colleague of mine kindly picked me up the next morning for work; we were due to train hundreds of educational staff. She asked how my evening was and I (quite matter of factly) told her: "It wasn't good actually, my close friend died". My colleague, not being Autistic but being Autism trained, said: "I know you'll still want to work today but you don't have to, and when I get back to the office I'll cross out this date in next year's diary as I know that's when it hits you."

We did our day's work – goodness knows how, but we did – and yes, a year to the day later I did not work at all and the grief hit me tenfold. It takes me a year to feel the sadness, the loss, the devastation, but I struggle to process and display it in a conventional way before that time.

This happens at happy events too. I watch women give birth on TV and they all tend to cry with happiness, a really ugly cry of sheer elation. I felt like that on the inside with my daughters, but I didn't cry. With my first baby I just gazed for hours in fascination, for my second daughter I went into super flight mode and immediately washed us both, put my jeans on and was home making dinner and bathing her big sister within two hours of the delivery. My third and youngest was premature and we were both in hospital for quite a while. I noticed how the other mums of premature babies were acting differently to me. They were reading magazines or talking to one another a lot. I was sitting in the hospital bed with my university books and laptop writing essays between pumping breast milk as I didn't want to miss a course deadline. The happy cry that mums do on television documentaries when they give birth did happen though, like clockwork, with all three of my girls: the minute I put them to sleep on the evening of their first birthdays.

Big emotional events take time to process, autopilot working and logistics fill up the space until then; I know many Autistic girls who have gone on to have careers that need this skill, becoming, for example, doctors and paramedics. I am sure their emotional processing, when it isn't misunderstood, can be an advantageous trait.

Let's also think here about the Autistic girls who are masking, copying and imitating to fit in, perhaps taking on whole new personas, alter egos and accents. How many of these Autistic girls' medical notes will be stamped with Dissociative Identity Disorder (DID) rather than them being given support for their masking?

What about the girls misdiagnosed with BPD (Borderline Personality Disorder), who are seen as anxious about being abandoned and impulsive and attention-seeking, when the meltdown in the supermarket that led to them being restrained by security was in fact sensory overload and the deep pressure sensory feedback the restraint gave was enough to help them through the event? BPD and attention-seeking, as they stopped when attention was given? Or Autistic and overwhelmed, and deep pressure helped?

I'm not a psychologist and it's not my place to diagnose, but as an advocate it is my place to give a different perspective, add a point of reflection and ultimately try to safeguard. I worry particularly for Autistic girls when they may be misdiagnosed, wrongly medicated and worst of all left with mental health records that do them no favours whatsoever as an adult Autistic woman.

It may be helpful to compare the symptoms of mental health conditions alongside the traits of Autism.

Let's look at typical traits of mania through the mental health lens:[10]

- Feeling very happy, elated or overjoyed

- Talking very quickly

- Feeling full of energy

- Feeling self-important

- Feeling full of great new ideas and having important plans

- Being easily distracted

- Being easily irritated or agitated

- Being delusional, having hallucinations and disturbed or illogical thinking

- Not feeling like sleeping

- Not eating

- Doing things that often have disastrous consequences – such as spending large sums of money on expensive and sometimes unaffordable items

- Making decisions or saying things that are out of character and that others see as being risky or harmful.

Now let's look at why an Autistic girl could be misdiagnosed with mania by looking through the Autism lens:

- Feeling very happy, elated or overjoyed – emotional processing delay of a happy event that now seems out of context as the timing is off?

- Talking very quickly – giving lots of information or "info dumping" about a favourite subject?

- Feeling full of energy – has rested or has created an environment which suits their sensory needs and wants to enjoy that at last?

- Feeling self-important – has had great success at work after many years of bullying at school and wants to own it?

- Feeling full of great new ideas and having important plans – maybe they have…?

- Being easily distracted – is ADHD in the mix? Having too many tabs open in the brain and feeling close to burnout?

- Being easily irritated or agitated – sensory issues, or poor environment?

- Being delusional, having hallucinations and disturbed or illogical thinking – having exceptional hearing and hearing REAL sounds that others can't hear (and so assume aren't real?)

- Not feeling like sleeping – melatonin issues?

- Not eating – wrong foods for sensory profile? Anxious and overwhelmed so controlling food?

- Doing things that often have disastrous consequences such as spending large sums of money on expensive and sometimes unaffordable items – help with budget skills needed? Special interest or expertise needing new "stock" to support it?

- Making decisions or saying things that are out of character and that others see as being risky or harmful – social imagination support needed? Victim of grooming, child sexual exploitation (CSE), mate crime?

Next let's look at BPD traits through the mental health lens:[11]

- Emotional instability – if you have BPD, you may experience a range of often intense negative emotions, such as:

  - rage

  - sorrow

  - shame

  - panic

  - terror

  - long-term feelings of emptiness and loneliness.

- Disturbed patterns of thinking

- Different types of thoughts, including:

  - upsetting thoughts – such as thinking you're a terrible person or feeling you do not exist. You may not be sure of these thoughts and may seek reassurance that they're not true.

  - brief episodes of strange experiences – such as hearing voices outside your head for minutes at a time. These may often feel like instructions to harm yourself or others. You may or may not be certain whether these are real.

  - prolonged episodes of abnormal experiences – where you might experience both hallucinations (voices outside your head) and distressing beliefs that no one can talk you out of (such as believing your family are secretly trying to kill you).

- impulsive behaviour, an impulse to self-harm – such as cutting your arms with razors or burning your skin with cigarettes; in severe cases, especially if you also feel intensely sad and depressed, this impulse can lead to feeling suicidal and you may attempt suicide.

- a strong impulse to engage in reckless and irresponsible activities – such as binge drinking, drug misuse, going on a spending or gambling spree, or having unprotected sex with strangers.

• Unstable relationships – if you have BPD, you may feel that other people abandon you when you most need them, or that they get too close and smother you. When people fear abandonment, it can lead to feelings of intense anxiety and anger. You may make frantic efforts to prevent being left alone, such as:

- constantly texting or phoning a person

- suddenly calling that person in the middle of the night

- physically clinging on to that person and refusing to let go

- making threats to harm or kill yourself if that person ever leaves you.

Now, let's consider those BPD traits through the Autistic lens:

• Rage – meltdown? Delayed anger over an event?

• Sorrow – delayed emotional processing over a sad event?

- Shame – over-thinking an event where they felt they got something "wrong"

- Panic – uncertainty and needs not being met?

- Terror – fear of past misunderstanding being repeated in a high-stress environment?

- Long-term feelings of emptiness and loneliness – long-term exclusion?

- Disturbed patterns of thinking – different patterns of thinking?

- People with BPD are described as having different types of thoughts, such as upsetting thoughts, affect them. Viewed through an Autistic lens, this could be a fair thought process if your life thus far has consisted of being told you are naughty when you are not, and being treated with exclusion as opposed to inclusion in the family home, classroom and adult life.

- Brief episodes of strange experiences – understanding that most people have an internal dialogue is vital for Autistic people to know. If someone was to ask me if I can hear thoughts inside my head I would answer yes. I can hear my own thoughts whilst typing this book; I can hear an internal dialogue when reading a book inside my head. Most people do. If an Autistic girl was to be questioned about voices inside her head in a clinical setting would she fully understand the context of what that question means and what her answer might mean to the professional?

- Prolonged episodes of abnormal experiences – sensory issues linked to acute hearing should be looked into prior to any questioning/observations of audio hallucinations. As a child I could turn the lights off, leave a plug on and still know which plug switch was on by sound rather than sight. I had sleep issues as I could hear the fridge and electricity in the walls. These were real sounds, without that context though it could be misdiagnosed.

- Impulsive behaviour – many Autistic girls sadly self-harm, for many reasons. However, for Autistic girls' self-harm may not be rooted in feelings of intense sadness, but be more closely linked to sensory seeking, feeling in pain so causing a greater pain to block out the many smaller pains, finding certainty in uncertain times, finding routine in uncertain times, establishing cause and effect when feeling powerless. We know Autistic women are far more likely to attempt suicide than non-Autistic men.

- A strong impulse to engage in reckless and irrespon-sible activities – Autistic girls are highly vulnerable to being misled by their peers, groomed, becoming victims of CSE or county lines child exploitation. They may be unable to spot a toxic relationship in a timely way, and struggle to maintain their boundaries.

- Unstable relationships: constantly texting or phoning a person – this could be due to hyper-focus on an indi-vidual. It could be that the Autistic girl was gaslighted or love-bombed by texts and calls from their abuser at the start of the relationship so they do not see these constant texts as an issue at all. Why would they in that case? It's how the other person approached them.

  - suddenly calling that person in the middle of the night (as above!)

  - physically clinging on to that person and refusing to let go/making threats to harm or kill yourself if that person ever leaves you – this should never happen: it is abusive. But if an Autistic girl was to say it, from what I've seen professionally over the last years, I'd be keen to know what films and TV series they have been watching recently. It may be that they have heard this said during a break up scene and so it is copied speech, and a way to convey their hurt (albeit badly).

Next, let's turn to Dissociative Disorders as seen through the mental health lens. Symptoms of dissociative disorder can vary but may include:[12]

- Feeling disconnected from yourself and the world around you

- Forgetting about certain time periods, events and personal information

- Feeling uncertain about who you are

- Having multiple distinct identities

- Feeling little or no physical pain.

And now, let's consider Dissociative Disorders through the Autistic lens:

- Feeling disconnected from yourself and the world around you – sensory issues, burnout, catatonia, shutdown, meltdown, emotional processing delay and being misunderstood can have this effect.

- Forgetting about certain time periods, events and personal information – being overwhelmed or masking to survive can do this too, temporarily.

- Feeling uncertain about who you are – so would many girls if they have lived their own life without knowing they are Autistic.

- Having multiple distinct identities – masking!

- Feeling little or no physical pain – interoception and sensory issues. As everyday life causes pain and distress (be it lights, sounds, clothing, food) the Autistic girl's baseline experience and therefore tolerance of pain is different to others'.

STRATEGIES AND TIPS

- Suggest the Autistic girl you support makes a diary of her mood each day and notes the events of the day. Ask her to write the best thing and the worst thing that happened each day. If you can unpick the patterns in her emotional processing time this will really help to strategically mitigate misunderstandings or distress for her with a long-term plan to predict her emotional support needs.

- Learn as much as possible about masking so you are well equipped to challenge a DID suggestion or diagnosis. DID is often a coping mechanism for someone to block out trauma or abuse. Its origin is therefore likely to occur after abuse has taken place. Autistic masking is different and could be from an early age and has no link to trauma. Autistic people will be aware they are masking, from what I've learned people experiencing DID often aren't aware.

    Consider this strategy backwards too, do you support any girls diagnosed with BPD or DID? Could it be they are Autistic?

- Mental health misdiagnosis "annulments". When an Autistic girl has been misdiagnosed with a mental health condition this can often leave an unhelpful legacy in her adult life. Professionals working with Autistic women should look deeper at the context of historical records. I believe an "annulment" of misdiagnosed conditions before the Autistic diagnosis was in place should be considered.

The problem with the educational system

Holly told me: "School isn't a place I can learn. I don't want to dip a toe in a subject I want to immerse myself in a topic for a year at a time; how can I begin to learn when I have to change topics, teachers and classrooms every 45 minutes?"

All Autistic students' needs differ. My own educational experiences and those of my three daughters, two of whom are diagnosed Autistic, all differed. Both my Autistic children are female, both have the same diagnosis, both grew up, raised by the same mum, in the same house, in the same decade, but they are two completely different young women with completely different educational needs and wants. One daughter was able to stay in mainstream education until about 13 years of age and the other stayed in mainstream education until age 10, but they both essentially ended up having to be home educated. One of my daughters went to a school that had a unit for Autistic students; this is a set up that I truly believe all mainstream schools should offer, not only as I found it a good model of practice for my only daughters but it has helped time and time again with many Autistic teen girls I support. I have seen the benefits of how add-on Autism units work, and the consequences for Autistic girls when this can't be offered in their local area. Autism units added onto a mainstream school don't always mean that's where an Autistic student would be supported all day. After all, we can't promote inclusion by being exclusive can we?

I've worked with educational settings for Autistic students, sharing and, more importantly, gaining great insights along the way. In 2017 I was lucky to team up with two friends, one of whom at the time was a director of CAMHS and another who was doing a PhD in Autism and Home Education (and who is now officially Doctor). We constructed, as a trio with more girl power than Charlie's Angels, a parliamentary submission[13] looking into mental health issues within schools in the UK. Thankfully, that submission was accepted and published and it's on the government website. I now help a lot of Autistic teens one-to-one with educational hurdles. That's important as an advocate, as I'm hoping not only to bring a perspective from growing up in the 1980s and 1990s (because I'm frankly ancient), but also to bring the perspectives of the young people I support today, with their modern experiences and school hurdles. Advocacy can't just be around my own and my family's experiences but rather it needs to incorporate the experiences of the people I support, both in my community and throughout the UK.

So how is mainstream school going wrong for so many Autistic girls?

There are grey areas of our educational system. Those in the mainstream, yet to be diagnosed, face an issue I'm assuming any educational professionals reading will come across all the time: where a student isn't deemed "disabled enough" to warrant the SEN provision, yet meanwhile they're not able to flourish in the mainstream environment.

Note that not all Autistic people identify as having a disability, I do identify as being Autistic and having a disability as it affects my everyday life; also I feel comfortable with the word Disabled and don't see it as a negative word. Views on this come down to individual choice though.

So, let's talk through a school day. I think others may well assume that the school day starts at 9am, when the bell rings and you go in, but for an Autistic girl it's different.

Before the start of school itself, it's almost as if Autistic girls have already completed a day's work and depleted their energy. In fact, the school day may well start from the night before. If I could dedicate this chapter to anyone it would be to the Autistic girls terrified on Sunday nights when they hear the *Antiques Roadshow* theme tune and who are having a panic attack, because I can remember being that child. The minute I heard the *Antiques Roadshow* soundtrack it was akin to Pavlov's dog, but the noise triggers the dread not food. I love that TV show. But it was that sign, that alarm-type bell for me, that told my replenished nervous system that the journey back into school was starting again.

I make no secret of the fact that I struggled with and left school at 15, without any GCSEs. I've been trying to make up for it since in a more vocational way.

So, imagine you've heard the *Antiques Roadshow*, your nerves are suddenly on flight mode and then you have to actually sleep? The night before school, sleeping issues could be fuelled by worry about what's going to happen tomorrow. Regardless of anxiety, Autistic girls often struggle with sleep issues due to different melatonin levels (some are prescribed melatonin to address this). As sleep is elusive in the first place, any stress or dread means it will be ten times as hard to get some rest before school.

When they wake, if they've slept, their mobile phone alarm rings, then the Autistic girls have to get ready for school. Sounds simple, but it isn't. It's not as easy as just getting dressed. Sensory issues around clothing (from itchiness of labels, through tightness to length and beyond) that can take vast strategies and time and patience to support arise.

One of the things that I see as a parent, and that I hear from speaking to other parents or families I support, is that there are moments of optimism. You get so used to living in an Autistic-friendly way that you could be forgiven for forgetting that other families experience the morning routine for school much differently. That bubble bursts when somebody who hasn't been an Autistic child themselves or doesn't have Autistic children says something at the school gates and, of course, it becomes clear that the reality of their journey to the school day is very different. I recall hearing a mum complain her child had only just slept through the night at six months old, SIX MONTHS?? "Try 12 years!" I wanted to quip back, but I just smiled and congratulated her. I wasn't envious; I also didn't sleep through the night alone until I was 12. So, to me, six months of age sounded like an unimaginable time scale anyway. For parents to hear that is one thing, but for Autistic girls who naturally feel a great difference, sometimes guilt and shame over not being able to cope with the sleep before school or school itself, comments like those can erode their self-confidence, especially in the school years.

It's worth professionals keeping in mind that the Autistic girl and her parent/carer will be exhausted before 9am. It's not as simple as just getting yourself dressed; there are many things to navigate. It could be the fact that they have run out of the only brand of socks that the Autistic girl can cope with, or that they have those socks but now the Autistic girl can't wear them because they've been washed in a different fabric conditioner, or dried on the washing line rather than the tumble dryer, meaning they feel completely different. This is, of course, if the school allows freedom of choice over the uniform with socks, shirts, skirts, blazers, hats and the like. Many schools don't.

Can you imagine having to take your child out of school because of uniform?

For parents and Autistic girls struggling to maintain these social norms and manage the expectations of the school system, simply getting out of the house and into school in the first place is often a feat of military precision.

Let's assume uniform is now on, we start thinking about the school bag and lunchbox. Autistic girls, diagnosed or not, are, in secondary school years, noticeable by something that often only other Autistic people spot: the neon flashing sign of the student wearing an overly weighed-down backpack. Why? Often an Autistic girl brings every single book for every single lesson they have that week in their bag.

Various reasons contribute to this. It could be that a heavy bag feels grounding and it's comforting to have a heavy backpack for sensory issues, or it could be that it's much easier to just take everything school-related each day as that way they don't have to try to remember what lessons are on which day, don't have the fear of losing their school things at home and ease the dread of being told off by their teacher for forgetting something (which, incidentally, often results in a detention and more time at school!). From that nerve-alive time on Sunday eve, through the sleepless night and during the anxious sensory school uniform morning, is there really the emotional and mental space to sort out books? Far too tricky to work out the timetable, especially if she's already exhausted.

If you're looking out for undiagnosed Autistic girls, who struggle with getting dressed and lack of sleep in the mornings so they just pack everything, it's that's heavy bag that's always a sign for me. Something for educational professionals to be aware of too.

Right, back to the school day, though we're still not at school yet: now comes the transition and the travel to school itself. If it's the walk to school – who is she walking with? Does the Autistic girl have trusted friends who live locally, or will she have to walk on her own? Will she get lost? Is she vulnerable to strangers or fake friends en route? What's the weather like? Is it raining? Will her clothes get wet causing her sensory hell to start again? Did she remember an umbrella? (That part may be more UK-specific!)

If it's a school bus or taxi to school – who else takes this bus? Kind students who will give her the seat she prefers to sit in? Bullies who will use this as a captive time to tease her? Is the taxi driver DBS checked? Is there a chaperone on board to ensure she is safe and protected? Will the bus or taxi be on time, every time? Will they be late, causing confusion and distress? Will it be the same driver or whichever driver is on call that day? Does she have her headphones in order to block out the hustle of loud voices?

Many Autistic teens I support don't want to wear their ear

defenders on the way to school because doing so basically makes them stick out like a sore thumb. They want to have their discreet earphones and music playlist playing instead. This can be a real deal-breaker. One of the Autistic girls I supported simply could not access school transport if her earphones were lost or broken; her parents quite literally had a drawer at home full of various earphone backups.

OK, so let's imagine our Autistic girl has now safely managed to travel to school and let's think about the sensory side of accessibility within a school building. We hear a fair bit in our media about accessibility and the built environment, be that gyms, offices, housing and shops. However, based on my experience of school environmental audits and visits, schools, even newly built schools, lag behind other buildings in terms of accessibility.

Part of my work is ensuring that the accessibility of Heathrow airport is of a first class standard for all. For an airport where you may spend a few hours before a flight, great care and planning goes into every design (be it new or historical) and everything is reviewed by panels of pan-disability professionals to ensure no one is left behind and those few hours before and after a flight are accessible for all.

So why aren't we doing this as standard for the buildings that an Autistic girl will spend five days a week in, from four to 18 years of age, and will make or break her access to education and therefore her chances of employment and independence?

If you visited a school and the young girl you were supporting used a wheelchair but couldn't access the classrooms as it didn't have ramp access, you would be shocked that was allowed to happen in this day and age. So, what about the Autistic girls who cannot access classrooms due to sensory issues that cause them great physical pain? Sensory issues are NOT a preference, a fuss, an irritant, over-sensitivity or being demanding. Sensory issues are an accessibility need that cause great physical pain and, in some cases, can risk life.

I recall an evening school visit to a brand new state of the art secondary school. Yet both I and the Autistic girl I was with couldn't last more than 15 minutes before having to walk out to safeguard ourselves from pain. Echoing walls amplifying what seemed like millions of whispering voices, screeching chairs on hard flooring that made us jump out of our skin, squeaking microphone announcements. The lights were small, energy saving lights, but there were literally thousands of these lights that were turned on both day and night. (I went back in the day to make sure. Ironic. So much for energy saving.) These lights shone with a sharp blue tint that was so sharp it felt like your brain was being stabbed by a hot rod via a (now useless) eyeball.

Can you begin to imagine trying to learn in such pain?

It may also be smells that the Autistic girl cannot bear; some describe smelling things so strongly it feels as if they are being force fed. Not too bad if it's delicious cookies being made, I guess, but what if the overpowering smell is the cleaning materials or compost and manure used on the school garden? Or it may be another sensory issue, such as the transition of temperature when having to change from uniform to PE kit.

Education professionals may notice for example that an Autistic girl doesn't attend school every Wednesday. Professionals need to play detective here. What happens every Wednesday? What is the trigger, the pain that causes her need to avoid school? Is she in a classroom opposite the canteen and Wednesday's menu consists of a strong-smelling meal?

Let's continue her journey through the school day with the assumption it's sensory-friendly. How is she managing to cope with her health needs in the school day? Many Autistic girls have differences in their awareness of when they need to drink water, not knowing they are thirsty. They may also refuse to drink water in the school day as they know they struggle with being aware they need to use the toilet in a timely way and don't want to have an embarrassing accident.

For an Autistic girl, the rest of the school day, if sensory needs are met, may be filled with the exhausting duties of maintaining social currency and keeping up with peers, whilst wishing away the remaining classes. It is not just tiring for the Autistic girl to engage with her classmates, it is also exhausting for her to say and do what is expected of her from the teachers. What if her teachers haven't had any training about Autism, led by Autistic people? At best their support for the Autistic girl will be misdirected, at worst it could border on abuse.

Gilly was 6 and attended a small village school in a highly re-spected middle-class area. The ethos of the school seemed to be, sadly, "fit the mould or we will break off your edges to make you fit" (or failing that, treat you so badly your parents remove you entirely). When her grandmother picked Gilly up from school one day she was wearing a green hat, and by hat I mean a long bit of green card stapled together to make what can only be described as a dunce's cap. On the hat was written in black marker "I will be polite to everyone I meet". Gilly had been told that the hat was not to be removed from 9am until 3pm and was to be worn at both lunch time and break time in the playground. It is impossible for me to understand the thinking behind this, and why the teacher thought it would help – to be frank, it seems like child abuse. Gilly's grandmother removed her from that "respected" school and she never set foot in it again.

Jessy was 13, at an all-girls school with a similar ethos. Being Au-tistic she didn't often make eye contact, and when she was really interested in a subject she would look away even more, so her ear was facing the teacher. This helped Jessy block out anything visual, avoid eye contact and learn. The teacher took a pile of papers from his desk and hit Jessy on the back of her head telling her: "you WILL look at me when I talk to you". He knew she was

Autistic and that she wasn't being rude, but was trying to listen with great respect and interest. When her advocate visited the school and offered Autism training for free, the headteacher's response was, "It's not what is wrong with our school, it's what is wrong with that child."

Why on earth would an Autistic girl feel safe in school after that?

Many parents are blamed and vilified when they ask their daughter's school for SEN (Special Educational Need) help, because if their daughter is subdued at school and only reacting and exploding with pent up frustrations when she gets home it is written off as a "problem at home". It's not, it's a problem at school too. Autistic girls will only unmask (see Chapter 3) when they feel safe, so if they feel safe at home that's where their frustrations and behaviour will escalate. If they aren't able to unmask at school, they do not feel safe in school, full stop. If you are a teacher reading this and you have an Autistic girl in your class who feels able to speak up, unmask, stim and sometimes explode, please (after playing detective to establish what could be improved for her in class) also see this as a compliment. It means she feels safe with you too.

STRATEGIES AND TIPS

Without singling people out, could the education professional build in a time (say 11am) when everybody is asked whether they would like to use the bathroom? Putting those routines in as a classroom rule would discreetly support those who need it.

How can we help our Autistic girl be understood in the school day? Professionals should keep in mind that what they see may not be what is happening underneath. Autistic girls are often much like swans, gracefully gliding above the surface but desperately kicking their feet to stay afloat underneath. As professionals ask yourself: is my student daydreaming, or is she processing, thinking and creating? Is she misbehaving, or is she in pain? Is she mixing with the wrong crowd, or desperate to fit in?

At all times, be a detective into what lies beneath the surface. If she seems to be unfiltered and talking to members of staff informally, be aware that she may not use social hierarchy in the same way as non-Autistic girls. It might seem that the young person has no respect for authority when actually she is very rule-driven and it seems like her actions don't marry up to her ethos and values. This struggle with hierarchy can lead to her being misunderstood, but differences in grasping hierarchy aren't always a bad thing. It might be the case that you have a young person who wouldn't understand the difference between speaking to one of their mates in the playground and speaking to the headteacher – it's going to be exactly the same type of discourse each time. But that's also a wonderful thing, because that student would also not be concerned about the difference between speaking to a king and to someone homeless on the streets. So, it's a lovely trait to have. Even though it's usually less understood, it doesn't make it wrong.

If you wanted to be able to teach the Autistic girl you support about hierarchy, maybe have a discussion (as a group class activity not just with her alone) about rules and explain why those rules are in place. Covering this explicitly will help her, because it's not going to come naturally.

Make your uniform policy accessible by making it flexible – simple.

Simple strategies such as ensuring they are sitting near the front, are not expected to make eye contact to be polite, are not sitting directly under a light or next to a window where they will be distracted or in pain, don't cost much; they just need a bit of consideration.

Think about their exams – context is required for all questions, be that in the classroom or in exam settings. The question is often a test in itself. Stating what they are being asked to demonstrate in explicit instructions can be incredibly helpful.

When I support Autistic girls heading for exams, I discuss exam questions and suggest they look out for the action words in the questions. Sometimes those words are underlined or in bold. I remind her that, if she gets stuck, to stop. If you have no idea what the exam question is asking, you look out for words that are involved in the question because the words in bold are normally words that you have to put into your answer.

When unstructured times arise, often schools will have something like a buddy bench, where, if somebody is alone, they can go and sit on the buddy bench and somebody will come up and ask them if they want to play or hang out. Actually, a lot of Autistic girls would rather have an un-buddy bench: time to be left alone in peace to restore and process before the next class. They may not really want to participate in playtime as they need some time to sit, read a book and chill out.

Some Autistic girls will find the playground inaccessible even to enter, so a good strategy is to offer inside calm and quiet lunchtime clubs. Themed clubs such as art, computer, or book clubs, work better than a neon-signed Autism Club, which, as they get older, they may feel humiliated to attend. Just host clubs around interests that they might have, so that way they naturally get to mix with other girls with similar interests and, often, similar neurodivergency.

Be vigilant looking for the signs of anxiety. That could be twirling hair or stimming more. It might be somebody who is forgetting their words again for sensory reasons but also forgetting to maybe have something to eat or have something to drink. Their distress could come out in all sorts of ways and result in meltdown or shutdown. The shutdown won't look aggressive, it will look very quiet, they will feel very sad and they will need you to find them a quiet area to be alone, where everything is dark. There is no gain to asking more of the Autistic girl at this stage, it's a bit like it being a piping hot day and putting your laptop in the conservatory, with 150 tabs open: the laptop just gets so overheated, overwhelmed, it turns off. And whatever you do, you can't turn this laptop back on and make it work.

All you can do is take it out of the heat and wait. That wait, and what it may look like, would be bespoke to that student. It could be as simple as just needing to go outside for some fresh air. It could be that they need to go home and recuperate. It could be that they go to the nurse's office, or access sensory tools such as a weighted, fluffy blanket. It will be different for each person, but if teachers are able to spot someone before that happens it is going to really help the Autistic girl in a healthcare sense as well.

We can't go on this way

In the Introduction I spoke about patterns, a timeless flow chart of the vulnerabilities an Autistic girl faces before diagnosis, or before support. So what are these patterns?

I am going to look at two scenarios in this section: what an Autistic girl's life has the potential to be with early diagnosis and support, and then the contrary.

Scenario one: Diagnosed, supported Autistic girl's life
PRESCHOOL YEARS

- Parents and professionals understand when the girl's sensory issues are overwhelming. She is given sensory breaks and a reduction in sensory overload so can live with much less pain and anxiety and gain confidence in the world around her.

- She has less fear of leaving parents, potentially.

- Masking may have already started, but parents and professionals raise the child in a culture of pride in Autism and let her know she doesn't have to hide her authentic self.

PRIMARY SCHOOL YEARS

- Teachers and the school are aware that they have an Autistic girl starting their school and refresh their training to make sure the environment is correct for her.

- The child feels cared for so fear of leaving parents to go to school is reduced.

- Bathroom breaks are scheduled in for the Autistic girl and her 1:1 (the 1:1 is best practice, but by no means a given!) so she gets used to using the bathroom in the whole school day, resulting in fewer accidents, no water infections and not being ostracized by friends.

- Her teacher understands that classroom requests must be specific so less embarrassment and misunderstanding for the Autistic girl.

- She is able to enjoy play time with less vulnerability and feel safer in the playground as she is supervised and supported.

- She may feel less exhausted after school, but even if she doesn't her parents have been taught strategies to make sure she can decompress and recover.

- She has extra support in school so she doesn't fall

behind on SATs and phonics tests; she has reasonable adjustments so she is able to attend residential trips.

- Although the end of primary school years sees a gap between the Autistic girl and her non-Autistic friends, it's been expected, planned for and any emotional and self-esteem disaster mitigated.

SECONDARY SCHOOL YEARS

- Masking isn't needed as she feels valued and secure at school.

- School refusal is rare; bullying and assaults are rare.

- She has a small group of trusted friends.

- Great Autism-tweaked sex education means she is more empowered over her sexual health and identity.

- She is less likely to be falling behind in school work, less likely to have an eating disorder, less likely to self-harm.

- Shutdowns are rare, catatonia is mitigated.

- She has support accessing GCSEs.

- Her relationships with boyfriends and/or girlfriends are loving and consensual so she is less at risk of CSE and less likely to end up in care.

YOUNG ADULT YEARS

- She is able to attend college or university with the right financial and pastoral support.

- Her fear of failure is recognized and reasonable adjustments are made so she can be tested and qualified in a way that does not strike fear and result in self-destruction. She is less likely to quit late into the course.

- She has been able to do her own research and has had support mitigating toxic relationships with many years of safeguarding support.

- She is able to find loving and unconditional friendships and relationships; she is less vulnerable when attending evening social events and accessing nightlife as she has kind and loyal friends.

- She still needs time to withdraw as she can be overwhelmed by life, but may be less likely to have mental health issues that impact her severely due to the support of those around her.

- Because her family and professionals know she has an Autism diagnosis, she may be less likely to be misdiagnosed and wrongly medicated for mental health conditions.

- She may be able to report abuse in a timely way or leave a toxic relationship faster; she may decide to not get married young.

MID ADULT YEARS

- She understands she may have different experiences of giving birth, but is aware she has interoception issues and does regular pregnancy tests each month to check she isn't pregnant.

- If she is pregnant and decides to continue the pregnancy she sees a midwife who has had Autism training.

- Understood in parenting style and motherhood, she feels confident in herself and doesn't struggle with the social aspect of the school playground pick-ups and drop offs.

- She feels able to work full-time and has financial independence because of this. She may find she stays in positions for a longer time (high retention rate).

- She may have health problems but professionals are aware of her Autistic diagnosis and recognize sleep paralysis could be shutdown or catatonia; excruciating migraines could be sensory overload etc.

- She may have been able to sustain her childhood friendships in the way non-Autistic women have managed to. She may have experienced loving and consensual relationships.

- If she has had to deal with legal proceedings in divorce and family law, this was handled with understanding.

- She has equal access to cervical smear tests; cancer screening issues are noticed before they urgently require treatment.

Scenario two: Undiagnosed and unsupported Autistic girl's life
PRESCHOOL YEARS

- She is misunderstood when sensory issues prove overwhelming.

- She has great anxiety and fear of leaving her parent.

- Masking has potentially already started.

PRIMARY SCHOOL YEARS

- Her fear of leaving her parent to go to school continues.

- She may not use the bathroom in the whole school day resulting in accidents or water infections.

- She often misunderstands the teacher's requests in the classroom.

- She is unsupported and can feel unsafe in the playground.

- She feels exhausted after school.

- She falls behind on SATs and phonics tests.

- She is unable to attend residential trips.

- The end of primary school years sees a dramatic gap between the Autistic girl and her non-Autistic friends.

SECONDARY SCHOOL YEARS

- Masking has peaked.

- School refusal, bullying and assaults occur.

- Her lack of friends leads to feelings of isolation.

- Boys assume the girl fancies them because she approaches without the same inhibitions as others, leading to sexual vulnerabilities.

- She falls behind in school work, develops eating disorders, self-harms.

- She experiences shutdowns and catatonia.

- Accessing GCSEs is difficult.

- She's at higher risk of teen pregnancy and may have older boyfriends.

- She's at risk of CSE and may end up in care.

YOUNG ADULT YEARS

- If she is able to attend college or university, she will have a huge fear of failure and may quit late into the course.

- She is vulnerable in friendships and relationships, and in evening social events such as accessing nightlife.

- She may withdraw and be overwhelmed.

- There's a high possibility of mental health issues due to lack of support and/or misdiagnosed mental health conditions due to her Autistic differences being misunderstood.

- She may be unable to leave a toxic relationship, and may be married young.

MID ADULT YEARS

- She may not realize she is pregnant and may have different experiences of giving birth.

- Her parenting style and approach to motherhood may be misunderstood.

- She may struggle with the social aspect of the school playground pick-ups and drop-offs.

- She may feel unable to work full-time and have financial pressures due to this. Trying to find employment that fits may mean she has a high turnover of jobs or she may prefer to become self-employed so she can pace her own working hours.

- She may be prone to health problems which professionals try hard to diagnose: depression and sleep paralysis, or shutdown/catatonia? Excruciating migraines or sensory overload?

- She might not have been able to sustain her childhood friendships in the way non-Autistic women have managed to.

- Her relationships may have been abusive.

- She may have misunderstood legal proceedings in divorce and family law.

- Due to cervical smear test hesitation/screening issues, health conditions may go unnoticed until they urgently require treatment.

In 2017, an informal survey which I posted online[14] asked for anonymous feedback from Autistic adults about the hidden cost of being Autistic, undiagnosed and unsupported. Sixty-five adults replied.

- 67% reported having no support in their school years.

- 89% reported having mental health issues that they feel they wouldn't have experienced had their Autism diagnosis come sooner in life.

My local authority's extreme lack of experience, training and support; no social outlets as in clubs and no money or funding to pursue them, makes for a child socially inadequate, bullied, beaten, assaulted. Which has resulted in more costly assessments, therapies, support that need not be happening; possible future independent living costs due to damage and late support. (Anonymous survey respondent)

- 89% reported leaving education without the qualifications that truly represented their abilities.

- 13% became a young parent due to lack of Autistic-inclusive sex education in school.

I left school with three GCSEs. I went back in my later years and got a post grad, so clearly capable; by then I'd spent years in minimum wage jobs. The isolation of being a carer to kids lacking support has damaged my mental health, making it hard to access the work force and use MY abilities. (Anonymous survey respondent)

- 81% reported having to rely on benefits at some point to survive.

- 97% agreed that more funding and support for Autistic people in the early years would in the long term benefit the UK economy as a whole.

My child could have been capable of work when they left school, had they been diagnosed sooner. They are on benefits. They were also capable of a university place and will not get one. This is a personal and economic disaster. (Anonymous survey respondent)

Whichever professional capacity you are reading this in, be it governmental, political, educational, healthcare based, legal, safeguarding or more, think about the hidden cost to the individual Autistic girl.

The hidden cost to the future children of the Autistic girl.

The hidden cost to the educational system and budgets, the employment and financial independence of the Autistic girl and society at large, the mental health system, the healthcare system, the benefits system.

Think about the hidden cost of the talents, skills and expertise lost to the country when we don't safeguard Autistic girls' education and life experiences from the very start.

CHAPTER 2

The Risk to Autistic Girls' Safety

Sexual abuse

I've found that many abused Autistic young women have such a cheery predisposition; they are possibly the most misunderstood young women of all. They smile and have a constant glass-half-full attitude from lack of experience or naivety. They have an eternal smile, hope and kindness because their life has so far relied on not much else but a smile stitched together with hope, spending most their days people-pleasing and pumping as much kindness into the world as they can in the vain hope that one day the world will learn to be kind to them in return.

From the outside you'd never guess that Nala was Autistic; perhaps even more unexpected was the fact she was always smiling, light-hearted and full of humour. Yet behind the Oscar-worthy brave face was a life so far of almost constant abuse.

When Nala was five, she was sexually abused by a now deceased family member. This abuse went on regularly until she was 11. Nala didn't know she was Autistic then and, once she understood that her parents didn't automatically know what had happened, she blamed herself that she hadn't communicated better with them, as they most definitely would have made it stop.

She didn't make her parents, or anyone in fact, aware until after the abuser had died and she was 15 years old. Her reason? She had one night prayed the abuser would die and a month later, from a sudden illness, he did. Nala was sad that she had caused him to die, so told her parents it was her fault he was dead and her prayer had worked – when of course the death was unrelated. Being unaware that her parents didn't already know the abuse was taking place had a wider implication for Nala. She assumed that it wasn't abuse she was experiencing at all – because if it was, her family would have stopped it, right? Her boundaries and expectations of how to be treated by men were at rock bottom. Abuse from others became an expected way of life so the list of sexual abuse and bullying from other men also became extensive. Having additional personal care needs also meant that her boundaries around her body were perhaps less than the average 15-year-old. If a young person still needs help and prompts to shower and wash, it's often that their experiences of privacy and boundaries will differ too. Red flags become pale pink.

How on earth could her parents have known she was being abused when Nala hadn't told them? Why did she think that?

Because Nala is Autistic, but was then undiagnosed and she struggled with understanding that her personal knowledge wasn't common knowledge until she communicated it. In other words, she assumed that because SHE knew, THEY knew – they didn't.

So, for seven years Nala was regularly abused, and unable to make it stop. Nala is sadly one of the individuals within the statistic that 91 per cent of Autistic adults have experienced abuse prior to diagnosis and support.[15]

I understand reading that statistic as a professional, parent or carer for an Autistic young woman is hard, so please let me quickly follow that up by a reminder that 73 per cent of the same pool of Autistic adults asked said that after diagnosis and support they either experienced no abuse at all or knew how to report it in a timely way. The fact you are reading this book and gaining support for the young person in your mind makes them leap into the safer category.

How can you ask for help if you don't know what help is?

Spotting abuse, or that someone may be abusive, is hard for any young female but can be even harder for Autistic females. Part of what makes up an Autistic girl's diagnosis of Autism, as previously discussed, is their social imagination differences. So, how can they really have the same ability to safeguard themselves in new events, experiences, places or with new people?

To understand what help means you have to jump some hurdles:

- Hurdle 1: What is happening is wrong, I'd like it to stop.

- Hurdle 2: Loved ones do not already know what is happening.

- Hurdle 3: How to communicate and share what is happening with a loved one.

- Hurdle 4: There will be an advantageous consequence to me sharing and communicating what is happening. It will make it stop.

The ability to talk in no way correlates to the ability to ask for help; even the most verbal young person may not know if, when or how to report abuse or ask for help.

Amaira was fantastic at sport, she came first in the cross country in PE and, on this particular school day, got a medal. On the way home she was mugged for her trainers. On her arrival home her dad asked "How was school today?" Amaira replied that the school day was excellent, waving her certificate to show her dad, then went to her room to process the sad event from her way home. She didn't tell him about the mugging: Dad hadn't asked about the journey home, he had asked about the school day itself.

Asking one daily straightforward question can help navigate this. An example of a specific non-leading question is: "Tell me the best and the worst thing that happened to you today?" Practise this every day. Join in and share your best and worst events of the day too; make it a routine discussion sharing smaller issues, so when larger issues arise it doesn't feel forced. Use times where no eye contact is required, sitting in school transport or side-by-side in the car facing forward. If talking is a no-go, use a diary, but find a way to ask this question every day.

When it comes to sex education, there needs to be a lot more done for Autistic girls in the classroom. Sex education is now compulsory in any type of school, but professionals do need to tweak that for Autistic girls.

There are a number of reasons for this. One is that Autistic girls may not understand other people's agendas. While that's true of many teenage girls, Autistic or not, Autistic girls are incredibly vulnerable to this because of their additional social imagination issues.

I wrote a free online course called "Bodies, boundaries, abuse and reporting it"[16] to try to highlight how Autistic girls may assume that their knowledge is everybody else's knowledge. If something has happened to them they may not report it in a timely way, which can leave them incredibly vulnerable.

Sex education is mainly taught in schools and, as many Autistic girls are home educated, sex education for Autistic girls also needs to be available online. This needs to be easily accessible to girls in or out of school as they have really significant challenges, especially around adolescence, and their risk of sexual abuse is very much overlooked.

Autistic girls are often infantilized and left behind when it comes to safeguarding lessons. Another adaptation that may be required is that, due to social communication differences, Autistic girls may take street jargon and metaphors at face value. I recall being in the supermarket with my 23-year-old daughter. It was a Saturday, and we were planning on chilling out that evening at home. I asked her loudly in the busy aisle: "Hey, do you want to Netflix and chill tonight?" My daughter, and half of the supermarket, were mortified by (my assumption of what was) an innocent question. "Mum, do you have any idea what Netflix and chill means?" my daughter asked. I didn't. I assumed it was a metaphor for watching films, drinking wine and eating popcorn; in reality in street jargon it means staying in to have sex. Luckily, born without an embarrassment gene, I thought this public misunderstanding was hilarious. My adult daughter however did not.

When I'd returned home and unpacked the popcorn ready for a now super-awkward movie night, I got thinking. If, as a woman in her late 30s, I made that mistake in understanding metaphor, what would the ramifications have been for a 19-year-old girl asking a non-Autistic 14-year-old boy at film club to "Netflix and chill"? Would he assume the Autistic girl was asking him for sex, which would, in the UK, be absolutely illegal?

What if it was a 13-year-old Autistic girl who received a "Netflix and chill?" text from the non-Autistic 17-year-old boy at film club? Would she not understand his (illegal) agenda? Would she think he really meant films and relaxing and agree to something she didn't consent to?

Imagine their fate in a court of law; without the best lawyers and personal assistants, how would they access a fair trial? It's a dangerous vulnerability, both personally and legally.

Whilst constructing the "Bodies, boundaries, abuse and

reporting it" online course[17] I asked the Autistic community for their anonymous feedback via an online survey.[18] Here are some of those responses:

> *All it took was for my parents to ask if he had touched my swimsuit area for the truth to come out, direct.*

> *Took me 25 years to disclose that I'd been abused. Then made such a mess of disclosure...blurted it out during a meltdown... that family didn't believe me for nearly a year.*

- 82% of Autistic adults asked said being Autistic makes it harder to report abuse in a timely way.

> *For me, thinking and especially talking about the abuse triggers a meltdown that makes it pretty much impossible for me to coherently tell my story.*

> *The worst abuse was from my mother but she lied and denied it all the time; I could not get away from her.*

- 78% of Autistic adults asked felt that some Autism "treatments" such as Applied Behaviour Analysis (ABA) increase the vulnerability of an Autistic person to abuse.

> *"Applied behaviour analysis (ABA) is a behavioural therapy which has the aim of changing observable measurable behaviour, usually by manipulating antecedents or using reinforcement."*[19]

In the "best" cases this is positive reinforcement and in the most abusive cases this is negative reinforcement. That, alone, is a safeguarding issue. What lays deeper however is that, even if an Autistic girl was given £1 million each time she gave eye contact or stopped flapping, making vocal ticks or rocking in her chair, she would have her most priceless safeguarding tool stripped from her: her ability to be non-compliant when she chooses to say no to an adult. Being trained to comply with an adult consistently as a minor is never going to give her the tools to fight back, say no, stand up, report and leave. Non-compliance is a survival tool for the most vulnerable. An outright ban on ABA and all other conversion therapies is needed; in my view, they are the same as conversion therapies for the LGBT+ communities. Not to mention that telling a vulnerable child who is going into a ruthless world that their body is there for neurotypical people to use as they see fit is an incredibly stupid thing to do. It leaves them open to anything from physical exploitation to sexual exploitation and sends them the message that the abuse is their own fault. Some forms of ABA are incredibly physical. How is a child of five supposed to tell the difference between an adult grabbing their face and slapping them? How is a child of five supposed to tell the difference between an adult pinning them down and an adult forcing themselves on them? It does not sit well with me. It's also telling that ABA advocates are never Autistic themselves. In fact, Autistic people are nearly universally against ABA. It speaks volumes.

Let's think about the social dynamics too.

If an Autistic girl has struggled to retain friendships with non-Autistic girls, I would bet my bottom dollar that around the age of nine or 11 an odd gap happened to appear between them and their non-Autistic girl friends. This is the point when friendships with girls change from fluidly having friends that aren't set in stone to a perplexing new situation where girls have to choose a clique, a best friend within that clique and chip away at their own uniqueness to fit the clique mould, which usually means they all end up having the same schoolbag and haircut. Time isn't spent on interests, it's spent on gossiping about each other.

Boys, on the other hand, are often a bit more straightforward in their communication. Observe boys from any age: if they don't like one another they have a fight, they have a scuffle and it's over. It's all done in front of one another, and is always very honest, maybe brutally honest, but it's honest. Conversely, girls have a tendency to whisper behind one another's backs, being what is called "two-faced". An Autistic person, male or female, is going to really struggle with that. So, Autistic girls may tend to have friendships with men, or boys, which for the Autistic girl may feel safer and more straightforward.

But then, of course, is the boy that the Autistic girl befriends assuming that she wants to be far more than friends? Is the boy aware the Autistic girl just wants friendship? What about the boy's intentions? Does he want to hang out with her because she's funny and kind and good fun? Or does the boy only want to hang out with her in the hope it leads to more? It may well be the case she just wants to be friends; it may well also be the case that she adores his friendship and also has other strong feelings for him, but dare not say in case she loses him completely. He would, if he has her best interests at heart, likely have to be very brave and ask her directly. If they both like one another just as friends, great. If they both like one another as more than friends, also great. But if one likes the other more: potential disaster.

Autistic girls, like any other teens, want to have friendships. Often for Autistic teen girls friendships come at a cost. The girl wants friendship, but the boy wants sex. Does she lose her only friend, or does she give him sex to keep him around?

The issue of friendship at any cost
What happens to the Autistic girl who surrounds herself with many male friends? What's the perception from the other girls in her year? Do they think she just gets on better with boys or do they see her as some teen boy-eating monster who is after their crushes? How does her male best friend act if he did fancy her and then discovers she has many male friends?

It's important that Autistic girls are safeguarded and taught about other people's perspectives. Many Autistic girls are home educated so online courses covering these issues should be available freely online as Autistic girls have significant challenges, especially around adolescence.

When we think about boundaries and an Autistic girl's right to say "No", it is important to remember that personal boundaries are not only for her body. We need to help Autistic girls learn to set boundaries for feelings, to protect their self-esteem and mental health. Every time an Autistic girl does something that she does not want to do, she can jeopardise her own feelings. Over a long period, she will sadly damage her self-esteem, happiness and even her long-term mental health. Autistic girls might not feel the consequences of this at the time, especially as many Autistic girls experience a delay when processing and feeling their emotions. Sometimes it can be days, weeks, months or years later before she eventually feels the effects of not being true to herself, and not saying "No" when she wanted to.

Being different and thinking differently from non-Autistic people is not a bad thing, it doesn't mean that her thoughts are wrong. However, because there are more people that are not Autistic than are, most of the people around the Autistic girl are likely to think in the same way as each other and only a few will think in a similar way to her.

This means that a lot of people can use their neurotype and their way of thinking to work out what someone else is thinking (just from knowing what they have said or done) faster than Autistic people can. For this reason, if the Autistic girls you support are unsure about how someone feels about them, or what their intentions are, encourage them to talk to their trusted adult and ask for advice.

Making assumptions about what information others have in their brains and what they can do based on what they know and what their friends do can stop Autistic girls from recognizing the unique skills and abilities she has. All Autistic girls have different talents and good qualities; not everyone is the same.

STRATEGIES AND TIPS
Technology that can help to safeguard

Technology is a wonderful way to keep the Autistic girl you support safe especially outside the home. A smartphone means an Autistic girl can text or call their trusted adult to stay in touch or if they are in need of help. There are apps Autistic girls can download onto their phones which can help them if they are lost and maps that can prove very helpful for practising walking through new streets.

As an Autistic adult myself, I tend to have difficulty finding new places, which leads to incredible anxiety. To prevent this anxiety, I try to learn where I am going by visually researching my route before I set off. I walk myself through a new street in the safety and comfort of my own home using Google Earth streetview, either on my laptop or phone. This can even be done with a cheap virtual reality headset. That way, by the time I have to travel to a new area I feel like I have already been to the new location and know what to expect.

Give her the permission and tools to leave an unwanted situation
The Uncle Kev trick

If the Autistic girl is in the street, alone and notices that she is being followed, a potential way to get out of the situation is to run. That isn't always the best idea, particularly if the person following them is going to get a sick kick from seeing a young girl terrified of them, although she may still need to make a quick exit.

The Uncle Kev trick is helpful in this situation. When being followed, teach her to wave at the nearest house and run towards that nearest house and shout "Uncle Kev". Why? The need to run is more likely to look like it is with excitement to see Uncle Kev when in fact it's a way to get out of the situation fast without the follower thinking he is in control and she is scared. This can deter the person following them, as they will assume the Autistic girl will soon be with an older family member. When she makes it to the nearest house this then gives the Autistic girl a chance to make a phone call or knock on the door of the house until the coast is clear and she is safe again. If this happens at night, make sure she waves towards a house that has a light on. Make sure she uses a different name to Kev, because now everyone who has read this book knows the Uncle Kev trick.

The emoji password

If someone in the Autistic girl's friendship group suggests an activity, such as a "dare", or a game she does not feel comfortable with, it's a good idea to prepare in advance a tool to help her make an excuse to leave the situation and/ or call her trusted adult to ask for help or advice. But this can feel awkward as a teen, as she may not want the group of friends to know why she wants to leave. Maybe she feels shy or not safe to "grass them up".

One tip is to set up a code word or emoji that she can text to her trusted adult. When the trusted adult gets this word or emoji by text, it will alert the adult and they will know the Autistic girl wants to leave the situation and be picked up urgently. The trusted adult can then call the Autistic girl and say that she must come home, or be picked up to be taken home, straight away. The trusted adult can also give the Autistic girl an excuse to tell the friendship group.

Best not to use the word lie here, as lying isn't always appreciated by Autistic people and the Autistic girl you support may refuse to lie to her friends. A discussion about the difference between the context of a lie and a white lie, keeping something secret and keeping something private could really help her navigate her safeguarding. There are times in life where we will all need to lie to safeguard ourselves or others and that doesn't make her or the trusted adult a liar consistently.

So what excuse/false reason/white lie could the trusted adult say, loudly, down the phone to the Autistic girl who has sent the password emoji or word to get her home safely?

- Bedroom needs tidying

- Homework has not been done

- Nan is visiting, and she wants to see everyone

- The dog's eaten the cat.

OK, perhaps not the last one, we all know it would be the cat eating the dog: totally unbelievable.

It is likely and understandable that as a trusted adult you will want to know why the Autistic girl you support needed to leave. This is because they need you to safeguard them and you will naturally want to make sure that they are OK. If you find your Autistic girl does not have the energy to talk at this time when she has been stressed and you know that she is not feeling able to share her reasons for leaving at the time, maybe you can arrange a "deal" in advance. For example, it could be the deal that, if the Autistic girl needs to use her emoji or code word, she will also be allowed a few hours in her room to concentrate on herself and her own feelings before sharing them and before being questioned.

Remember, as a trusted adult it's hard to step back and not immediately ask questions. But be happy to know she is safe and learning to make good choices to safeguard herself.

Do not let anyone else know that you both have an emergency emoji or codeword, or what it is. Just as you would not share your bank card PIN, or talk about it, your emoji or codeword has to be kept out of public knowledge to work and keep the Autistic girl safe.

Talk to your Autistic girl about whether she will be allowed or will still want to carry on seeing the people she was with at the time you used the codeword. It is important she knows that using the codeword won't automatically means she is banned from those friends, or there's a risk she won't use it at all.

However, understand and share together that, if the situation she needed to escape from was very serious and if it is in her best interests, long-term, not to be with the group again, as trusted adult you might ask her to stop seeing them in the future.

If, due to social imagination differences, Autistic girls can't easily see an advantageous result or consequence to their own or others' plans, can they really enjoy those plans? Can they really be cautious enough with those plans?

Let an Autistic girl know her rights!

The United Nations Rights of the Child clearly displays the rights that ALL young people in the world have. Regardless of the country you live in, your disability, race, or gender, you have these rights. Many young people, Autistic or not, are unaware of their human rights. If you read through the list of human rights with the Autistic girl you support it goes a long way in helping her to understand boundaries, because it is clear to see why some unwanted actions against young people are neither ethical nor legal.

However, it is a sad fact that many human rights exist only if WE act upon them. Human rights are a set of ideals that are created and agreed by human rights professionals, workers and then by countries who adopt them, they aren't always the law.

After looking at the list of human rights provided by the United Nations, can you suggest an art activity for the Autistic girl you support to draw, paint or sketch any human rights that are most important to her personally? Can she think of an event or news article she may have seen/heard/ read that is not respecting the rights of the child?

Teach body autonomy as early as possible

If the Autistic girl has higher personal care needs, you don't have to take away her power or consent. Let's say, for example, she needs help putting her socks on: ask her what sock she would like to go on first, the right sock or left sock? The outcome is the same, two feet with socks on, but her control and sense of body ownership empowerment is different.

Avoid, at all costs, ABA or any therapies that rely on teaching compliance. Any therapy that teaches or commands an Autistic girl to be compliant to a therapist or adult is bad news for her long-term safeguarding. If she is conditioned to allow adults to have control over her body and her reactions, how can she enter adulthood understanding her body belongs to her and her alone?

Remember not all those on Autistic support social media sites will be telling the truth, some predators fake being Autistic to gain the trust of very vulnerable children, their parents and the professionals who support them. As professionals, support staff and parents we must remain vigilant to what information we share about an Autistic girl we are supporting with other adults. It's not professional or safe to gain off-the-record advice from an Autistic adult posing in a mentor role. Only seek the advice of an Autistic adult if needed in a professional capacity by finding a fully insured, safeguarding trained, DBS checked advocate. Do not cut corners to save money – it is far too dangerous for the young person to do so.

Bullying and mate crime

The transition from primary school to secondary school was not going well for Jessica. The friends she had at primary had either gone to other secondary schools, or the ones who went on to the same secondary school had been hijacked by the much "cooler" and less socially awkward girls. Jessica was however popular with the older boys in the secondary school, which she enjoyed as they made her laugh and it meant she had people to hang about with at lunchtime. She considered them friends; they considered her easy prey.

One evening on the long walk home from school, one of the boys suggested that Jessica should not walk home alone, after all it was dark, and she was 12. He insisted he walked with her. The entire trip consisted of mild mocking which she viewed as harmless messing about. When they approached a concrete floor, he purposely tripped her up and shoved her face first onto the concrete. She lost her adult front teeth as a result and had to endure years of painful surgeries, bone grafts and dental implants as a result.

Charlotte was excited to be a part of the cool group of girls at 15, they had rarely paid her much attention before but had done more so in recent months. They were having a get together one summer in a field near their school and invited her to join the outside party. But there was no party. Charlotte was beaten up by a group of over 10 girls. She had been set up for months by the gang with a view to abusing her. Charlotte thought they were friends.

Bullying and mate crime devastates the self-esteem of Autistic girls, shattering their trust in others and making it difficult to trust again, or setting them up to experience false friendships and patterns of abuse again and again.

Mate crime is effectively a false friend who seeks a vulnerable person to befriend while having an underlying agenda to exploit and abuse them. It could be someone who only visits the vulnerable person on pay day knowing they will buy all the food and drink. It could be someone who wants to suddenly be friends with the Autistic girl after she has moved out and found her first flat, with a view to using her home as a place to stay rent free. It might mean making an Autistic girl pay all the costs on a shopping trip, cinema visit or the like, but never returning the favour. Constantly asking to borrow money which is never paid back. Maybe the Autistic girl you support has become far more popular since she passed her driving test, being used for lifts that her friends never pay fuel costs towards? Maybe the Autistic girl you support is unable to drive and friends who do drive are her way of gaining independence away from home, but they charge her astronomical sums for the lifts and taking a taxi may have been cheaper?

Technology has helped many Autistic girls have greater independence; however, it is really important to remember Autistic girls' safety online and help her set boundaries for her own wishes, rights and online life. Social media can be a fantastic way for an Autistic girl to talk to friends from the comfort of her own home, to find out more about Autism, her interests and her ambitions.

Social media is full of kind, supportive, friendly people. However, it is also a place that people who have unkind plans and intentions can easily upset someone. Some do this by mistake, and some do this on purpose – because they enjoy it.

Does the Autistic girl you support use WhatsApp, Twitter, Facebook, Snapchat, TikTok and other social media? There are some people online that will put pressure on Autistic girls to take part in "sexting" or ask them to share inappropriate pictures. This is often one of the first requests paedophiles use to groom children. Normally they offer to send them gifts or money in return.

Please bear in mind that the person who is asking an Autistic girl you support to send a photo may not be who you or the Autistic girl think they are. Even if they have been chatting online for ages and they seem really nice, they could be a lot older than they say or could have someone younger involved acting as a middleman.

Gwen was a young, pre-teen Autistic girl. During her time in hospital with a broken arm she was befriended online by an older teen girl who gave her lots of attention. The older teen girl started buying Gwen gifts worth hundreds of pounds and sending them to her. She wanted photographs of Gwen. Gwen sent them as she felt she had to. When Gwen finally got home the teen girl wanted them to meet up, but her parents said no and contacted the police after checking her phone. Later, it transpired that the older teen girl was not a girl, a teen or permanent UK resident at all, and they fled the UK when they were reported to the police. Gwen thought she was being given gifts by a teen girl she met online but, in reality, she had been groomed and it's likely she had just escaped from human trafficking, at 12.

STRATEGIES AND TIPS

- Be on the lookout for sudden, new friendships.

- Be vigilant if the Autistic girl you support no longer has as much money for her care needs, interests and bills as she did before.

- Be vigilant if the Autistic girl you support also suddenly has a hugely expensive phone, trainers and designer clothes and bags.

- Discuss what friendship in its truest form really is and delicately talk about what being used can look like.

- Remember to educate the Autistic girl you are supporting that ANY photo sent in a private message is no longer private once you press "send". It is highly unlikely that it will remain private, even if she thinks she can trust the person she sends it to.

Teen pregnancy

Zoe came to the office smiling from ear to ear one day and said "Mum's probably already told you but I'm going to have a baby." Zoe wasn't pregnant yet, but the emphasis was on the word YET, she was planning in great detail on getting pregnant as soon as possible, which was worrying as she was 13 and Autistic.

Zoe isn't the only Autistic girl desperate to be a mum whom I've supported over the years. I haven't enough fingers or toes to count them on, but she was certainly the youngest.

When we hear of teen mums, we assume a "mistake", but for Autistic teen mums, it's naive of us to assume all pregnancies are unplanned. Many Autistic teen mums may well have planned their pregnancies – many have told me outright that this is the case. That's often the focus of the work I do with Autistic girls, the preventive part. Up until now the strategies I use have had a 100 per cent success rate – well, at the time of writing anyway! So why do they want a baby?

The reasons I've come across are varied and broad but often include:

- a craving for someone who will always be with them

- someone to love them unconditionally

- a way to leave school and leave the childhood years of confusion, bullying and fear behind once and for all

- a protective factor (see Chapter 3)

- a way to leave home, especially if they are misunderstood there; imagining the placement care home or mother and baby hostel to be a 5-star hotel experience (it's not, trust me, I've been there).

It's quite hard to talk about teen pregnancy for personal reasons.

The personal reasons being that I have a 23-year-old daughter, and I'm 38 (feel free to do the maths on that one!) and there's a limited freedom on what you can say as a protective mum about a journey that isn't just your journey alone; my teen pregnancy was and remains my daughter's narrative too.

It's also a challenge to discuss teen pregnancy in the context of specifically Autistic teen mums as it's not just Autistic teens who may become pregnant and, obviously, every young person who ends up becoming pregnant is going to have a different outcome.

Some Autistic girls might decide to go through with that pregnancy and raise the child. Some might choose termination, some might choose adoption. You can't really round up the whole experience, so I'm going to have to talk more about what makes teen pregnancy different for Autistic girls. How does motherhood, if that's the journey taken, differ too?

Unplanned pregnancy

Let's start by stating what is obvious to most (but not to all): AUTISTIC GIRLS HAVE SEX, just like any other girls, and often sex results in pregnancy.

If we are thinking about unwanted or unplanned pregnancies, they could occur for many reasons. It could be due to a loving yet immature relationship; it could be due to safeguarding issues: the rape or abuse of an Autistic girl that's been disguised as a relationship by the abuser. We have spoken previously about social imagination and understanding consequences and other intentions so bear that factor in mind.

On top of which, an Autistic teen girl, if she also has high care needs, will have different boundaries around her body. Her boundaries will be different to her peers who don't have a disability and haven't had to share private moments of their life with another person for the sake of their own health issues. It could be the case that some teens still need help with bathing, toileting, even something as simple as toenail cutting. The way that the Autistic teen girl's body is treated and the way that she allows her body to be treated are bound to be different. This still of course does not in ANY WAY make an Autistic girl at fault for any abuse; the fault is solely that of the abuser.

So, good sex education and safeguarding materials do need to speak about the difference between a body being seen or touched for a health reason or a medical reason, and being touched for a reason which really doesn't benefit them at all. That leads to understanding body boundaries and the body boundaries of others.

I've worked with many older Autistic girls who have asked for support gaining a suitable contraceptive. One thing an Autistic young women told me, which I had never actually thought about before, was that she cannot bear the sensory side of condoms and has an allergy to a coating used on contraception pills. She opted for an alternative contraceptive method in the end, but it got me thinking about sensory needs and condoms, because it might be the case that sensory-wise condoms are just hellish, defeating the object of an activity which is meant to be pleasurable!

In the heat of the moment, a condom may not be used if it causes either sexual partner acute discomfort and pain.

There has been research into whether Autistic people are more likely to have HIV, because of sensory issues and condoms,[20] and although that research was based around the gay male population, it set off a dot-to-dot in my mind and my thoughts led me back to thinking about preventing teen pregnancy and Autistic girls.

Autistic girls and their access to abortion

Keira's parents, upon discovering she was pregnant, took her to a support service local to them for pregnant teens. It wasn't what her mother expected though. It was clear to Keira's mum when she entered that the agenda of this service was to try to convince her daughter not to seek a termination despite her incredibly young age. Keira wanted to stay.

Keira told me about an ice cream tub full to the brim of thousands of tiny balls of scrunched up paper with a sign saying: "This is how many babies are killed by abortion in one day".

They didn't use the word pregnancy, they said baby. They didn't explain how different a pregnancy looks at nine weeks to nine months. Kiera didn't leave with balanced advice to help her reach her own conclusion, she left having been convinced.

After her son was born, Keira was sent to live in a mother and baby hostel away from her family, in awful living conditions, dropping out of school and gaining no GCSEs.

Termination, however, is not an option for all. This may be for religious or cultural reasons, but may also be due to the fact that many Autistic girls didn't know they were pregnant at all. If I had a pound coin for every Autistic girl who told me they didn't know they were pregnant until much later (indeed some not until the birth!), I'd be a very rich lady.

Why is this often connected to Autistic girls?

Interoception is understanding, feeling and processing what's going on inside of us in a timely way; it can affect knowing if we are thirsty, hungry, in pain or pregnant (as explained further in the discussions on healthcare in Chapters 3 and 5). Autistic girls have challenges with this as part of their Autistic sensory profile.

Autistic women face unique challenges in both pregnancy and childbirth if their Autistic needs are not recognized, discussed and appropriate support implemented. Autistic girls who decided to continue with the pregnancy need understanding and support in labour.

Autistic women may feel reluctant to come forward to discuss their condition due to a fear of stigma and misunderstandings with healthcare professionals and social services. Their fears are rational: one in five Autistic women has been referred to social services, some experiencing the removal of a child.[21] Thankfully, in recent years, Autism and Autistic women in general have been better understood than ever before, leading to fewer misunderstandings in healthcare and social services. The legacy of stigma is, however, vast.

Nevertheless, it is imperative that Autistic women do come forward to discuss their condition as otherwise their very natural, Autistic patterns of behaviour can be misconstrued and misunderstood by health professionals. During pregnancy and labour, Autistic girls will also need someone to advocate for them at this most vulnerable time.

Examples of misunderstandings

- An Autistic woman uses medical terminology and has done research online about her pregnancy and then uses exclusively medical jargon in meetings with GP/ midwife. As an Autistic person it is natural to prepare and practise speech but it can be misunderstood by professionals as being a "know it all", "fake", "making it up" etc.

The predictable outcome to this is being viewed as rude/impolite.

- The Autistic mother becomes agitated at appointments running late as she needs more time to process what she's being told.

- An Autistic woman is confused about her regular appointment as she was told "next Wednesday" when she called up on Monday so she turns up two days later, rather than Wednesday the following week.

Examples of why Autistic women need specific Autism trained staff in labour
PAIN RELIEF

- An Autistic woman may have a very high pain threshold or not show her pain even when in great discomfort; she will need someone to know when she's in pain and to discuss pain relief. Autistic women find it hard to ask for help.

- Autistic women in labour may also refuse any pain relief as it's her last means of control over a very unpredictable event. I participated in The University of Philadelphia Autistic Women and Labour research "Childbirth Experiences of Women with Autism Spectrum Disorders in an Acute Care Setting"[22] where issues of communicating needs with nurses in childbirth were a strong common thread of occurrence.

SENSORY ISSUES IN THE DELIVERY SUITE

- Bright lights can cause extreme pain for all Autistic women and even fits for those Autistic women who also have epilepsy. Broken, flickering lights will cause dangerous levels of pain, stress and physical reaction.

- Sounds, sights, touch and temperatures may have an unexpected reaction.

- An Autistic mother may not cry with happiness when her child is born, this must not be seen as a sign of lack of attachment or empathy. This is mostly due to emotional processing and being shutdown post-birth.

I applaud any identifying process and support of Autistic women in pregnancy and labour for these reasons.

HOUSING

The hidden cost to the baby, the Autistic teen mum and to society as a whole is the housing issue of teen pregnancy. As someone who was once a homeless Autistic teen mum, I know on a deeply personal level the vulnerability and negative experiences faced by mums and babies in homeless hostel situations. It's a factor often overlooked by Autistic girls who want to get pregnant. If they struggle with social imagination, establishing the full gravity of consequences and imagining future selves, it's easy to imagine "having a baby" means just that. You'll get a bump, you'll give birth and then push a baby in a pram.

When my own daughter was about three months old, I noticed that her face started to change from that of a newborn to that of an older baby; she looked so beautiful. I remember also one Sunday morning having the stark realization that she wouldn't be a baby forever; that this time next year she would have had her first birthday and probably be walking; that a few years after that she would be at nursery and soon after be a schoolchild.

I hadn't thought that far ahead when I was pregnant. It didn't come as a disappointment, but it was a shock and just something I hasn't considered before. After all, I was told I was "having a baby", not a schoolchild who needs a home, family and providing for in a way like no other. I worked three jobs and created stability for her, but she missed out on me, and I missed out on her.

STRATEGIES AND TIPS

Where possible, try connecting Autistic girls in a safe and professional capacity with an adult who once was an Autistic teen mum. Sometimes Autistic girls will take on board the advice from someone like them, who's been there.

Suggest contraception before they become sexually active, if possible. If the Autistic girl you support would prefer the predictability of when to expect her periods open a discussion about how the contraceptive pill can help regulate her cycle. This has two benefits. First, she may want to regulate her cycle to help give her certainty and may choose to do that even if not sexually active. Second, should she choose to become sexually active but is too embarrassed to ask to be put on the pill, you have given her the best excuse to ask – she will now not have to disclose to you she is planning on having sex, she can simply ask to regulate her period and get the pill that way. When it comes to sexual health, condoms are obviously just as important. If you empty lots of condoms out of a box into a tub in a shared bathroom cupboard in the home that is a discreet way of helping out. If you have a sealed box of seven condoms and one goes missing, it's pretty obvious and not giving the Autistic girl the privacy she may need. Far better to have loads of different condoms in a large jar where no one is going to notice one or two missing.

The five-year plan

A strategy I use with the girls I support is to make a five-year plan chart. We literally chart out the year and age they are now, where they would like to be, what they would like to achieve in the years coming up, and discuss how they could reach their goals (academic or otherwise). Underneath this chart we make another showing the age of a would-be child alongside their age and how their goals, be they academic, arts, sports-based etc, would be affected by their new-found responsibilities.

For those who are already pregnant, NHS support and advice about options is needed so the girl can make her own decisions in an informed way. Avoid exposing her to religious doctrine, or other sources where a single point of view may be presented.

For the Autistic girls who continue their pregnancy professionals must be aware that their emotions may take time to process. Post-natal depression may be delayed too.

Get your office a Melody. Not a song, but a reborn doll. In my office you'll find a car seat, a bag of baby clothes, nappies and pram – and Melody the reborn doll. Melody is unlike a child's doll, she is a rather expensive hyper-realistic doll. Parents often look at me quite stunned when they pick up from appointments and I open the door with a "Congratulations, Nanny and Grandad!" passing them Melody and all the equipment. Normally I whisper, "Don't ask, I'll email you, enjoy!" And wave them goodbye.

I have found a good success rate with Melody. The Autistic girl gets someone to love, someone to take everywhere. They get the enjoyable side of having a baby (which does not suddenly grow up unexpectedly!) and they get the support and friendship of the other Autistic girls I work with at the office. Fortunately, the office I rent has a small private park with swings. Many of the Autistic girls now have their own reborn dolls that they bring to club. They hold birthday parties for their babies, take them out to play together and get that love and Autistic understanding they were yearning for somewhere safe, and away from less understanding onlookers.

Melody has been on holidays, to the beach, shopping and, frankly, has a far better social life than me.

In time, whether the Autistic girl is 14 or 20, the pram, car seat and Melody always come back, and more importantly the Autistic girl gets her future back. Job done.

Radicalization and gangs

Molly: there was something different about this young person which I couldn't put my finger on as I was standing on stage giving a talk on statistics, health and Autism in a government department capacity. I couldn't understand why this talk would be of interest to a young person who was clearly there alone and not in their job role. Why would such a young person be here in a posh Surrey hotel in the middle of the day, mid-week, if it wasn't to support a family member or as part of their studies or apprenticeship?

I continued to deliver my presentation and afterwards made my way back to my table. Molly had moved to sit next to me. She asked me for my email address as her Autistic friend was in trouble and needed my help; I was scared of running late to catch the train as I needed to pick my girls up from school, so I handed over my email, smiled and left.

It wasn't long after that I received an email from Molly explaining her "friend's" plight. Molly's friend happened to be Autistic, extremely good at technology, coding, website creation and the like, and had unknowingly been working for her pals as a favour helping to make their websites. The pals she worked for, however, were extremists.

This was the first time in advocacy that I experienced the torn feeling of how far you are willing to go to protect the vulnerable versus how far you are willing to go to act in the appropriate line of duty.

Ultimately, I had no choice but to report what I'd been made aware of and placed my hope, faith and trust in the authorities that the young person with a disability would be cared for as the gang's scapegoat rather than pinned as the mastermind. I later found out that this trust had, fortunately, been rewarded.

I was glad I left the issue in the hands of the authorities and, as guilt-ridden as I felt for having to pass information on about a vulnerable young person, I did what was best in the pursuit of national security and tried to forgive myself.

Many years later, by no connection whatsoever, I was fortunate enough to be commissioned to help write and review the Department for Education and National Autistic Society's guidance for Safeguarding Autistic Youths,[23] part of which was in regard to the prevention of radicalization. I noticed in my internet research for this project that many websites warned: "speakers may be approached at speaking events" – no shit, Sherlock!

STRATEGIES AND TIPS

- Prevention is key.

- If isolation, a desire for a group of friends, and a young Autistic girls' talent in technology could make her vulnerable, let's do our best to make them her assets!

- It's imperative that Autistic young people are made aware of how their Google searches could be perceived. For example, an Autistic girl who wants to go shopping for the ingredients to make herself bath bombs for a sensory experience and types "how to make explosive bombs", followed by Googling the opening times of her

nearest shopping centre, could end up in hot water –
not the nice warm bath type!

(This also goes for protecting her parents' red faces
when Googling "sexy teen boys" in her dad's work
laptop, which may not go down well with his boss
either.)

- Discuss these perceptions in frank, light-hearted,
  humorous and candid ways in school PSHE classes for
  everyone's sake.

- If any Autistic girl I come into contact with has a talent
  for coding, hacking her pals' social media accounts,
  building computers and the like, I signpost them to fun
  communities and projects who will unleash her talents
  in a safe and legal way – with likeminded peers. Keeping
  her safe from those who prey on talented Autistic girls.
  The Smallpiece Trust and GCHQ run a project called
  Cyberfirst.[24] I have signposted many Autistic girls here
  with great success.

- The National Autistic Society and the Department for
  Education also have a comprehensive guide to prevent
  radicalization in their July 2019 materials online.[25]

- If prevention is not possible and you are aware of any
  breaches to national security you should report this as
  soon as possible.

Note to other professionals – if at any point in your career
you are also asked to write guidance on preventing radicalism
and you work burning the candle at both ends, resulting in
you researching materials at 3am, for the love of God make
sure you post on your work website, Twitter, Facebook and
LinkedIn what you are currently researching and Googling. I
can't tell you how anxious I felt Googling terrorism and right-
wing extremist-based papers in the small hours for several

months, assuming the front door would be kicked in at any point by those who monitor the cyber world. The upside however was that I made sure the house was spotless – just in case.

Domestic violence and child marriage

In my role as an Autism advocate, I have supported many Autistic girls and young women who at some point, or many times, became victims of domestic abuse.

The abuser is the one to blame, so this section won't talk about how to aim strategies at Autistic young women, but will explain how domestic violence often occurs for longer for an Autistic young woman and ways we can work together to help an Autistic young woman escape.

As professionals we need to have a frank discussion about abuse via the Autistic lens to have a better chance of preventing the Autistic girls we support being victims of such dangerous and negative experiences.

It may be wise if we run through some different terms for different types of abuse and how these may have different implications and therefore require different strategic approaches for Autistic girls.

Physical abuse

Physical abuse is any intentional act causing injury or trauma to another person using bodily contact.

RAPE AND SEXUAL ABUSE WITHIN A RELATIONSHIP

Sexual abuse and rape can and sadly do happen within established relationships and marriages. The illegality of rape within marriage was laid out under the Sexual Offences Act 2003. (As late as 2003?!) If the lines between consent and non-consent have, in near history, been blurry for the non-Autistic among us, can you imagine what challenges face the Autistic girls and young women who may have additional hurdles navigating what the expectations are in a relationship and what constitutes abuse and rape?

Emily was one Autistic young woman who didn't understand that rape could happen within a marriage. Married young, without a peer group, she had no supportive network of women to vent and gain advice from – her husband was her entire life: her best friend, carer, crush, lover.

He had a high sex drive, she didn't.

Emily would often wake up to him having sex with her when she was asleep. When she asked him why he was always doing this he explained it away using the jargon "it's just morning sex". Struggling to understand this explanation but trusting her husband, Emily took it at face value.

Morning sex however is mutually agreed. Both participants need to actually be awake and fully conscious in order to consent to sex. This wasn't morning sex, this was routine rape. Abuse like this can be reported at any time, no matter how long ago it took place.

Financial abuse

Financial abuse commonly involves withholding information about household finances, controlling access to personal/joint finances and creating financial obligations in the name of the victim either without their knowledge or through coercion. Financial abuse is part of economic abuse which involves interfering with a partner's ability to acquire, use and maintain not only money but economic resources (such as housing, transportation etc) more broadly. This makes unravelling the extent of financial obligations post-relationship extremely challenging.

Being financially linked to an abusive partner post-separation can also be dangerous.

One common experience is the use of a victim's address for years after the separation.

It is often the case that, when the woman attempts to leave the relationship or marriage, the financial abuse becomes most dangerous. Endangering not only a woman's mental health but her credit score and future. How can a woman responsibly move on to a new relationship or even just an independent life when every financial resource she has is taken hostage? She can't move on and that's ultimately the control her abuser wants.

Becky realized with hindsight that financial abuse had taken place within her marriage at many times, but it was at its most intense when she left her spouse.

Becky took the brave move to leave her husband and assumed that would be her chance at freedom.

Her ex-husband, Ricky, aware the marriage was ending, took out loans on their previous marital home, purchased cars (which he defaulted on), refused to pay towards the mortgage, stopped maintenance for his children and took out overdrafts, loans and mobile phone contracts at the address. Becky assumed this would calm down and didn't know where or how to report it. Their children, like Becky, were also Autistic. She couldn't move home whilst they were small. The effect of so much change to their routine would have been just as catastrophic as the divorce. She didn't report his wrongdoings but went ahead to petition for divorce.

Ten years later, even after he was forcibly removed from the home's title deeds by a judge, Ricky was still in a pattern of gaining loans and sending red letters to Becky's home.

As unimaginable as it is, the abuse was at least consistent and predictable and she knew deep down that the moment any perceived financial gain was gone, so would Ricky be gone.

Becky's children needed routine, a stable home life, access to their school and a father in their lives even at this huge personal cost to herself.

Becky waited until her children were adults to scrape back her credit score and gain courage. Becky was able to move on, both literally buying a new home and emotionally drawing a line on the previous decade-and–a-half of feeling like she was living in a virtual cell. Along with her gift of freedom, however, her greatest fear was realized: without a financial incentive to stay Ricky no longer maintained his relationship with his children, although at least now they were adults.

Coercive control

Coercive behaviour is an act or a pattern of acts of assault, threat, humiliation and intimidation, or other abuse, that is used to harm, punish, or frighten the victim.

Controlling behaviour is a range of acts designed to make a person subordinate and/or dependent by isolating them from sources of support, exploiting their resources and capacities for personal gain, depriving them of the means needed for independence, resistance and escape, and regulating their everyday behaviour.

Naomi struggled with losing things regularly; she had ADHD as well as being Autistic. She noticed at the start of her relationship with Ian that she was losing things more regularly than normal but brushed this off as a consequence of being in a bubble of happiness and preoccupied with her newfound happiness.

Her phone went missing only a week after he moved into her flat. She decided it had probably become mixed up when he was unpacking his things and thrown out with the recycling.

A month or so later she made a great contact at work. Her male colleague gave him her number so they could liaise further about opportunities. When she wanted to call him on her phone, it was nowhere to be found. She was sure she had accidentally left it in her car but returned to the flat and found it under the water at the bottom of the bath she had just got out of, destroyed. She kicked herself for being so stupid to take her phone into the bathroom.

It wasn't until six years and eight lost or damaged phones later that she realized the pattern. It was Ian who had been destroying her phone and work opportunities each time something positive happened, each time she got a new friend or a new number.

Ian admitted to this in court when they divorced.

Charlie experienced coercive control as she was about to marry Neil. It was a whirlwind wedding to her soulmate.

She wanted to look her absolute best for him. He was beautiful, a model by profession, and she wanted to feel just as beautiful in their wedding photos.

Her usual weekends when she was single consisted of going to the gym or to nightclubs with friends and since being with Neil those activities had been replaced by staying home alone together, watching films and eating curries or pizzas.

Charlie didn't really enjoy nightclubs for sensory reasons – the hustle and bustle of crowded places was too much. She was as in love with her routine as she was in love with Neil. She had however gained weight and lost confidence. Due to be married within a year, she decided to kickstart her diet by using food replacement shakes and going for long runs after a full day at work. Neil was aware of how hard Charlie found working a full day and how being Autistic meant she loved their quiet nights in together. Neil was so caring he would have a bubble bath waiting for her when she got through the front door and wouldn't let Charlie lift a finger.

Neil decided she should rest and when she got out of her bubble bath, he would routinely make her meal replacement shakes for her ready for dinner time. Neil knew Charlie loved routine and would do the same every night.

Charlie's weight got worse rather than better. She was bigger than she had ever been and when she asked Neil or her friends why she was struggling to lose weight they just smiled and said it was due to being happy at last.

Charlie later found out Neil had been purposely making her 2000 calorie weight gain bodybuilder shakes as opposed to the 200 calorie diet shakes.

Charlie married him anyway. She couldn't break the routine she had grown to depend on and couldn't imagine life without him now.

Rachel had been with her girlfriend for about four years when she started a new evening college course, making friends with intelligent women who shared her interests and whom she felt she could be herself with. The college girls often went out at the weekend and although this wasn't always Rachel's cup of tea she trusted these new friends and made the bold choice to go out after four years of mostly being at home with her partner. Rachel was really excited and spent the day shopping for a new shirt and jeans and new makeup. Rachel's mum offered to dog-sit so her girlfriend could go out with her friends too, if she wished.

As they both got ready for their respective nights with friends, Rachel couldn't find her makeup or new clothes anywhere. Searching the entire house, they were nowhere to be found. She was disappointed, thinking she may have left them on the bus home, sad as she had wasted her money and that not only did she now had no make-up to help her feel confident, she also only had her boring old clothes. Rachel decided it was best to not go out. Luckily her mother had arrived at her home and drove her to the shops in the nick of time, buying her replacements as a gift. When both Rachel and her girlfriend had gone out to their separate events, Rachel's mum decided to make herself useful and help around the house. As she took the clean laundry out of the washing machine to dry it she found Rachel's new clothes and make up soaking wet wrapped inside a towel and hidden from her by her girlfriend. Rachel's mum told her the next day. Thankfully Rachel and her dog were welcomed back into her mum's home so she could leave her partner. It was just as well as her girlfriend didn't come home at all that evening, having decided to cheat on her instead! Lucky escape.

How might an Autistic young woman experience domestic violence differently to the general population?

- Change is extremely difficult for Autistic women. Transitions such as divorce and moving home are almost unbearable.

If change is your worst fear, staying in an abusive relationship may feel (as awful as it sounds) preferable to going through the stages of leaving.

Mix this with the struggle to know how and when to report abuse in a timely way, and the logistics for women like Becky, who are Autistic themselves and carers for Autistic children – in Becky's case this left her feeling she had nowhere to go, even if she did seek help.

- The abuser being viewed as the carer. There is a very fine line between care and control. All too often from the outside these can look identical.

If an Autistic young woman finds intimacy hard to maintain in a long-term relationship and the sensory side of daily sex difficult, is it OK to touch her and have sex with her when she is asleep? Or is that rape?

If an Autistic young woman has anxiety leaving the house and her partner insists on being by her side when she goes out in the evening is he caring or controlling? What if she wants to go out with her trusted friends and needs a break?

If an Autistic young woman with a history of eating disorders and working out daily gains an excessive amount of weight due to a rapid lifestyle change, and later wants to attempt a sensible diet to be a healthy weight, is it caring for her partner to regularly contaminate her food without her knowledge? Or abuse?

If any Autistic young woman struggles to make friends, is it caring to destroy over eight of her phones whenever she tries to make friends? Or abuse?

When it's written down on paper it's easy to see, but in the epicentre of the storm it's anything but clear cut.

- Perhaps being Autistic makes someone more vulnerable to gaslighting – being told and convinced their experiences are wrong, fictional or invalid – due to taking words and intentions at face value and having a life history of feeling you are the one to blame. If your perspective of events has been constantly undermined, you accept blame more easily.

If from childhood an Autistic girl is told "The music in the car isn't too loud you're being silly!" When it actually feels as if her ears are bleeding due to sensory issues, would she be more likely to just accept that she makes mistakes when she's told by an abuser that her perceptions are wrong? Professionals working with Autistic girls need to validate and believe their experiences of events right from childhood.

Cuckooing

Cuckooing is a practice where someone takes over a person's home and uses the property to facilitate exploitation. It takes its name from cuckoos, who take over the nests of other birds. There are different types of cuckooing:[26]

- Using the property to deal, store or take drugs.

- Using the property to undertake sex work.

- Taking over the property as a place to live.

- Taking over the property to financially abuse the tenant.

Child marriage

Are we ready to talk about Autistic girls and child marriage yet?

Too late, we are!

I have always strongly believed that the legal age of marriage in the UK needed to be raised. I think it's a disability issue as much as a cultural one. As recently as early 2021 the legal age for marriage was 18, and if that wasn't young enough, with parental consent you could have your child married off at 16. Thankfully this is currently in the process of being changed to make it illegal for under 18s to marry in the UK, but is 18 still too young? When we hear of such young brides you may imagine arranged marriages, cultural backgrounds, a power struggle between a child bride and a much older groom. We seldom imagine a similar-aged couple with hidden disabilities, or a disabled girl marrying a man who will take over her care. You may not imagine a teen mum who wants to make her family proud above all personal cost, or a youth who's transitioning between being in care to being in her first home and struggling without support.

I once listened to Rose, an Autistic woman, give a speech about how she had a marriage annulled. I was intrigued by this. I didn't know what the difference between a divorce and an annulment was.

Rose explained in her keynote that the groom she trusted and married forced her and her wheelchair-using child to live solely in the tiny utility room of her home whilst he and his gang of friends had the rest of the entire house (HER and her child's house, that is) to use for parties. Rose and her child escaped and later regained their home.

The more I open up about teen marriage to other Autistic professionals, the bigger the picture of unhealthy, toxic, abusive marriages prior to adulthood becomes.

STRATEGIES AND TIPS

- Support your Autistic girl to learn about what makes a healthy relationship and a safe marriage. Explain what the legal implications of marriage are and that she has a choice to remain in a relationship unmarried should she choose to.

- Training on domestic violence for all young people should be part of PHSE lessons if possible. Being able to understand the terminology and identify the red flags of a toxic relationship is vital.

- Every Autistic girl will grow up to be an Autistic woman. Many will have positive relationship experiences. Many Autistic women meet genuinely kind partners and are able to navigate parenting and dating or new relationships extremely well.

- Suggest to the Autistic girl you support that before committing to someone on a legal, cohabiting or marriage level she does her research and doesn't rush in.

  In an ideal world that would mean their love interest would formally apply by submitting a DBS check and two references from their past employers...in this imaginary case, their exes.

  Probably a bit much to expect!

CHAPTER 3

How to Identify a Girl at Risk

Masking

Imagine you've been invited to watch a show at the theatre; it's not a pantomime, it's serious theatre. During the show an usher taps you on the shoulder and marches you to the stage in front of the audience. The play doesn't stop, it carries on and the actors wait for you to say your line. There's a pause; they are getting annoyed, you don't know what to say so you just say anything that comes into your head. They react in a disappointed way, cross even. The improvisation continues because the other actors have been rehearsing this for months, they have the lines and they seem to all know what's coming next. You haven't any of these tools – you just came to observe, you're trying your best, but now you're in the thick of it and you are doomed to get it wrong. Now imagine that feeling every day for 32 years because life is a stage for which I never have the script. When attending school, when dating, when working, even when buying a pint of milk at the shop. And you can't make it stop, you can only try to observe as much as the scene allows and hope you get the gist of what's going on, that your improvisation skills don't annoy others and, at best, pass as adequate.

That's how I opened up my first ever conference lecture to about 400 doctors, psychologists, and multidisciplinary professionals – I didn't know then that the experience I was describing is known as masking. I also didn't know then I was Autistic!

So, what is masking?

Masking is where an Autistic person attempts to pass as non-Autistic by suppressing their authentic character, suppressing or disguising their stims – for example by sitting on their hands or flicking their hair rather than flapping their hands, or by dancing and fidgeting instead of rocking in their chair. Staring at others, looking away, blinking more, leaning their head on their desk, removing their prescription glasses or wearing sunglasses inside to avoid eye contact.

It can also mean copying other people that the Autistic girl idolizes, loves, respects or looks up to as "getting it right" in life. Autistic girls can copy their friends' mannerisms, accents, jokes, outfits and interests as a way to try to fit in or simply remain undetected as different.

Accents can be a wonderfully helpful tool if the Autistic girl has an appreciation of the arts and enjoys acting. A way I often communicate is by sending YouTube clips of television show and film scenes that I feel sum up an emotion or situation perfectly. Sometimes I learn scripts from film and television by heart and will reply vocally or by text using that script when I struggle to find the right words myself. Most people refer to these stock replies as echolalia rather than masking though. If it's masking that's behind the sudden accent change, however, this ability can get an Autistic girl in real trouble with those who don't understand.

Just ask my dad. He has a tale of me being a young child and every Saturday when we went to pick up a Chinese takeaway, I noticed that the chefs would speak to the customers in English yet would talk to one another in Chinese. I felt sad that they had to work so hard to communicate with their customers so took it upon myself to copy their accent and speak to them in a Chinese accent instead, much to Dad's horror. I was soon banned from picking up the takeaway.

Masking from the outside looking in seems like a great skill, and at times it can be. We become natural actors, performers and even great spies. The benefits of our talents at masking are usually for others though.

This one of the many reasons I detest the phrase "mild Autism". There is nothing mild about growing up losing your own interests, talents, likes and dislikes, eroding your own self-identity, sense of self and inner principles, all in order for other people to experience you in a way they feel comfortable with.

Mild Autism does not mean a straightforward life experience; it's means the non-Autistic people around the Autistic girl experience her Autistic presentation mildly whilst she herself implodes into a life of emptiness, depression and confusion coloured by vulnerability from constantly seeking self-approval from others.

Parents of Autistic girls will often struggle to gain support for their Autistic daughter at school, college, university or even within the clinical setting of diagnosis because the girl has used her intellect to self-strategize and mask.

Parents are then blamed for any issues, criticized for their parenting, and offered parenting courses. If the "problems" only present at home and not outside, they are automatically viewed as the cause of her issues.

Wrong, so very wrong.

An Autistic girl will likely melt down, shut down, explode or implode only where and when she feels safe. Think about that phrase: where and when she feels safe. If an Autistic girl is only able to show her authentic Autistic self at home, the parents are doing a first-class job at giving her a safe home life. It is therefore likely that school, college, university, family events or even the clinical setting is where she feels she has to mask.

It's the clinical setting that needs an Autism Course, not the parents.

Masking has been linked in research to poor mental health, self-harm and suicide in Autistic girls. As professionals we must give Autistic girls a safe space in as many places outside the home as possible. I would highly recommend the work of Assistant Professor Sarah Cassidy on masking.[27]

STRATEGIES AND TIPS

- Learn about masking, what it looks like and how to spot an Autistic girl who is shape-shifting and losing her own identity in a situation or environment. How can that environment be adapted to make her feel safe and comfortable to portray her authentic self?

- Can professionals support the Autistic girl to build up her self-esteem? If she is still unsure of her sense of self and sense of identity, that could be due to a late diagnosis and a life of masking. If the leap between idolizing others and appreciating herself is too big a jump, start small. Give her someone like herself to look up to until she learns to appreciate and recognize something good in herself. Perhaps if you are aware of any interesting relatives or historical links in the Autistic girl's family you could have a discussion about them and maybe do research as a project for her. Using worksheets that are about self-identity and interests is always a great way to build her confidence and help her unpeel the various layers of characteristics that she has felt she needs to copy in order to get by in life.

- Clinical assessment teams should be aware that the Autistic girl that visits is likely to be masking when she visits the clinic. Diagnosis may therefore take more time, more appointments and different environment observation than expected.

Drink and drug use

Jasmin is Autistic, but, like so many, is as yet undiagnosed. She found it hard to mix with peer groups and girls her age so often preferred the company of boys, mostly older, and started to use drink and drugs to ease her anxiety, fit in with the crowd she found herself in, and cover up her Autistic ways and need to stim. After all, if you are drunk anything goes, right?

By the time Jasmin was 11 she was smoking and drinking. At 13 she was using poppers and dodgy shop-bought supplements. By 14 she was using weed, speed and cocaine. Her mock GCSEs were sponsored by a mixture of the latter two of these, snorted in the school toilets as she was dared by her "mates" to see how fast she could write that English essay with chemical aids. She failed the exam, but the next class was dance and her teacher was so impressed with her moves he gave her a lead in the school play.

But how could a working-class girl not of working age afford such things?

Being given them free by the local dealers. And by free, I do not mean without cost.

Drug dealers don't tend to have gangs based on loyalty, good-hearted intentions or fabulous friendship attributes. Dealers have a harem based on fear and violence. They mimic a family style unity in an age-old pattern we know from Fagin, the Artful Dodger and Oliver Twist. And of course they rely on the addiction of gang members, whose reliance on what they are selling is all part of the gang leader's long-term agenda.

These gang leaders approach Autistic girls posing as a

protective friend who will stand up for them against the bullies at school, deterring the cliques who treat the Autistic girls badly and mock them – older men being the one force that the mean girls' boyfriends are petrified of. Suddenly, the Autistic girl is no longer bullied, teased or treated badly because she's now one of the gang. This has gone beyond playground politics. This has evolved into the serious and dark underbelly of adulthood.

The patterns are always the same. The Autistic girl feels untouchable to start with, until the honeymoon phase of fun and games ends; it's not long until they are addicted to whatever drugs their adult "pals" are sharing with them, not long before they are told they have to find ways to pay them back.

These Autistic girls end up in the most unthinkably vulnerable situations, all in order to remain part of the perceived friendship group, which is in reality a criminal gang.

The transactions vary. Autistic girls are often in sexual relationships with their 25-year-old "boyfriend". Some girls are dressed up to look older and taken to nightclubs, telling parents they are staying at a friend's house, not their boyfriend's flat, somehow allowed into clubs despite being about 14.

The clubs that won't body search girls are the main targets for the "boyfriend" as, on the way to their "date" he will take her to one side and stuff her bra with pills and cocaine for him to later retrieve from her mid-dance, so he can make his deals. Win-win for him: if she gets in unsearched, he can deal; if she gets searched and arrested, he can use her as a scapegoat and find another girlfriend.

Quite the gentleman – he sounds like a keeper.

This happens to hundreds of girls UK-wide, not to mention internationally, Autistic or not, but being Autistic can make it harder to spot agendas quickly. Being Autistic also means it's more likely she'll want to gain one up on the school bullies by seeking a place to fit in elsewhere, and be unable to understand, promptly, that the boyfriend isn't a boyfriend and that she is being abused.

Jasmin isn't a girlfriend. Jasmin is a non-consensual drugs mule, Jasmin is a victim of child sexual exploitation, county lines, and she is at serious risk of harm. Why? Because she wanted to feel safe, wanted the bullying to stop and wanted to fit in.

Jasmin got lucky. She escaped not just because of support from professionals, but because in this situation with her older boyfriend she became pregnant and, although life became challenging in a different way, Jasmin got what I've often heard in court proceedings noted as a "protective factor". Getting pregnant ultimately saved her life because she got out of the gang alive, has no criminal record, got herself sober at 15 and has never used drugs since.

STRATEGIES AND TIPS

- Create less isolation for Autistic girls by encouraging them to attend youth clubs and activities where they will meet likeminded friends in an Autistic-friendly environment. If they need to finish school early or be given less homework to be able to have the social energy and not burn out, then so be it. If there is not such a club in the Autistic girl's local area seek funding for travel or consider starting something Autistic-friendly closer to home.

- I use "What's the Debate?" cards[28] when teaching Autistic girls about the gritty subjects they are facing. The "What's the Debate?" cards cover topics such as child sexual exploitation, drugs, smoking, mate crime and more. They are cards with myths about the subjects on one side and facts on the reverse. I think they are marvellous and I definitely do not get paid to say that, I promise.

- If an Autistic girl is already mixing in these gangs and unable to get out, it's time for urgent social services and police support via the Multi-Agency Safeguarding Hub (MASH) teams.[29]

- Time to get the five-year plan out again and help them look at the consequences of being this gang's mule and underdog.

   "So, you want to perform in America one day? That's a shame if your 'boyfriend' gets arrested and blames you (which he will). A criminal record will mean no visa to the States I'm afraid, even if you're really the victim" helps give perspective on the gravity of the situation they have been put in.

   It's important to remember that although the older 20-something year-old-male is definitely acting illegally, he may too be a victim of a much wider county lines issue and with support could probably not only help the authorities crack a drug organization but could also do with a means of escape for his own life too.

Eating disorders

Sasha was 19, and had lost a dangerous amount of weight over the past 18 months due to a very restricted diet of broccoli and low-calorie snacks. Her glossy dark wavy hair was straw-like and there were patches at the front where it thinned. Her teeth were crumbling; her periods had stopped; her olive skin was now pale and discoloured. Sasha however had never felt better; for the first time in her life, she felt powerful. This was not about being thin; this was about control and empowerment. In a world where nothing was predictable, resisting food became her last act of control.

   Her recovery, like the start of her eating disorder, was in no way linked to how she felt about physical appearance. It was about self-esteem and autonomy.

Traditional methods for treating eating disorders may make Autistic girls with an eating disorder worse rather than better. Often those with an eating disorder are met with more demands, more restrictions, and less control. This won't work well.

The Autistic girl's drive to gain more control needs to be handled more carefully than a hostage negotiation situation – giving them fewer restrictions, fewer demands and more control. It's a risky task.

Food restrictions come early in life for many Autistic girls, often due to sensory issues.

Imagine you have five crisps (chips for my American friends reading). Every crisp you pull out of the bag will likely be a similar taste, size and texture.

Now imagine you have a bag of small tomatoes (or should I say, to-mate-oes). Every tomato will likely have a different taste, a different size, a different texture; some will be riper than others, some will explode in your mouth more than others. Unpredictable little blighters, tomatoes, aren't they?

So, is an Autistic child fussy? Only eating unhealthy food? Or are they, in their constantly unpredictable world, using food as a way to create a baseline certainty over what they eat?

Often professionals and well-intended family members will say, "only give them the foods you want them to eat, they won't starve, they'll eat when they are hungry!"

Big massive No!

An Autistic person won't eat if the only food on offer causes them distress. And many Autistic people don't know when they are hungry anyway (see the section on safeguarding in healthcare in Chapter 5 for more on this).

Let's think of the inpatient eating disorder mental health

units for those who need to be hospitalized to save their own life. I've been fortunate in the past to act as an environmental auditor of such wards and units. There are some, but still not enough, that are explicitly for Autistic girls who have an eating disorder. The ones I have visited in person as an auditor are, quite frankly, brilliant. Every effort has been made to ensure this distressing experience is made as comfortable as possible:

- Air conditioning and heating have been installed to be as sensory-friendly as possible.

- Kitchens are as "smell proof" as possible to ensure the cooking doesn't have an overwhelming effect on the nose and make an Autistic patient feel force-fed like some poor foie gras goose.

- Images that could be triggering have been removed from the walls.

- In one particular setting there used to be a canvas in sepia of a packed suitcase. It was nice and artsy, but do you really want a reminder you've been packed up away from home when you're at your most vulnerable? Likely not!

- Bright coloured photos and framed posters have been put in a box (alongside this suitcase canvas) so that they aren't on walls when someone arrives. If they'd like artwork on their walls they can bring their own or choose one they feel comfortable with from the box.

Doesn't sound like much does it? Think about it though, they are given CHOICE, control and empowered to decide what they visually digest. That's the choice, control and empowerment they are currently seeking by abstaining from eating. More choice, more control, more empowering elsewhere is the tipping point between recovery and a downward spiral to starvation.

I had an eating disorder in my 20s. It's not something that ever leaves you, it's always there waiting to pop up and be your mate in unpredictable times. While writing this book I was also in the process of moving to a new house – it was a busy and stressful and unpredictable time, and I found myself losing weight. Although I hadn't been starving myself, as I was finally able to see my hip bones again, I felt the temptation to gain certainty in an uncertain time rear its ugly head once again. The temptation is to count calories, weigh myself daily and have personal weight loss goals to gain a sense of feeling empowered and in control at this anxious time. Luckily, I know how to self-strategize to make sure it doesn't progress:

- no scales

- no weight goals

- no connecting the emotional weight I feel to the physical weight I feel

- and most of all: my special interests.

I hate to say "use special interests" when talking about Autistic girls as it feels often that our special interests are seen as a superficial add-on to our condition. They aren't often taken seriously, too often used to coerce us into a non-Autistic person's agenda – but they are our purpose, our passion, our friend, our safe place. Sometimes they are our careers and provide expertise that will lead to our financial independence in adulthood. In the meantime, they save our lives.

Looking back to my 20s, this was a useful strategy. At the time I was selling teeth. Not literally going around the streets with a bowl of teeth under my coat, that would be creepy. I worked as a saleswoman in a private cosmetic dental clinic. I had the best boss, who I still stay in touch with today. Female, feminist, owner, business woman, Doctor and empath rolled into one. She taught me that you could be a female, unashamedly smart, work in a caring profession and be empowered. I liked working for her very much.

One day she introduced a sales chart. The staff member who made the most sales that month would be made the "Sales Queen"; we all thought it was a bit of harmless fun.

That chart likely saved my life. I had a new way to feel empowered, new numerical data to concentrate on that was not calorie based. With as much determination as a marathon runner out on the track each day for seven hours a time, wanting to mildly torture themselves with a new personal best, I quickly became the office sales queen and a sensible weight. I guess I will never know if that's the reason my boss made the chart, or if the data was rigged in my favour and the whole team were in on it (knowing my ex-boss, that's likely!). But either way I didn't have an active eating disorder.

Thinking about the Autistic girls you support, what could help them gain that sense of empowerment? What do they enjoy? Gaming online? Photography on Instagram? Horse riding competitions? Sports? Acting? Could they have a new non-calorie-based numerical goal that gives the feedback on their success?

STRATEGIES AND TIPS

- Involve and connect to eating disorder professionals as soon as you feel it is important to do so.

- Think about special interests as a way to give the Autistic girl control and to lessen the reliance on food resistance to deliver this feeling of empowerment.

- Seek out eating disorder in-patient units that have Autistic-specific wards.

- Give the Autistic girl as much empowerment and choice

in her life as possible and lessen any demands. Even if that is school. There is no point having grades if you starve to death before you can get the certificate.

- Let them eat whatever they want, where and when they want. At this stage it does not matter what they are eating, if it is on their bed not the dinner table or at an ungodly hour. All that matters is that they are eating.

The common scapegoat

It is all too easy to label an Autistic girl who is in a pattern of being at the centre of many negative events with many different groups of friends (using the word friends extremely loosely here) as the common denominator. If we do not understand the pattern of events through an Autistic perspective, it's not always clear to see the Autistic girl was not the troublemaker or the ringleader, but more likely the scapegoat.

I would go as far as saying that if the common denominator happens to be an Autistic girl, she is not the ill-intentioned mastermind behind the negative event, and will not be solely to blame, if at all. Why?

Because as one Autistic girl, Daisy, described it to me, "Life is like having an 'I'm a mug' sticker on your forehead that everyone can see but you!"

I once watched a documentary about a gang of American teen girls who were in jail for life for robbing a house and killing someone. These girls were rightfully handed the force of justice, but there was one girl that I somehow knew from the minute I watched her on screen that she shouldn't be handed a life sentence. She described how she had no idea why these girls had called her for a lift, they weren't particularly nice to her at college and they didn't ever invite her shopping or to parties, but she was asked to help as they needed a lift and she thought they wanted to be her friend. She said she had no idea they needed a burglary getaway car and no idea whatsoever that they would kill someone.

So, what happens when the Autistic girl's character witness steps up in a murder trial and is asked if the Autistic girl is often in trouble?

Actually, yes, all the time, not just with these new "friends" but she is in a pattern of being involved in all sorts of events – she is the common denominator.

This doesn't start suddenly with an event as extreme as being in the wrong place at the wrong time, helping girls from college with a lift and then ending up with a life sentence for murder. This starts in childhood.

Daisy is Autistic. She has an elder sister. Her sister would always bite her when their mum wasn't looking. One such day with her arms covered in new bite marks beneath her shirt, Daisy decided enough was enough, time to bite back (literally). She had her mouth open just about to land when she was caught by their mum. Mum was naturally furious with Daisy's behaviour and she was sent to her room whilst her elder sister was comforted and believed.

Why didn't her sister tell their mum the truth? Well, because she would have also been in huge trouble!

Why didn't Daisy show her mum the bite marks on her arm from her sister? Because she is Autistic and assumed her mum already knew.

Who was found to be the troublemaker? Daisy. Justice is often not about who did it, but about who gets caught.

Now think of that progressing out of the home and into the primary school environment.

Polly wanted to make friends and decided to ask to join a group of girls who were playing in the school's wooden castle shed; they agreed.

Later that day when she was picked up from school, the teacher told her mum that she wasn't playing nicely in the castle and there were reports from the other girls that she was ruining their game.

Once home, her mum asked Polly what type of game they were playing together. Polly said, "A kicking game." Horrified, her mum sternly told Polly that kicking is not a nice game and she is disappointed she would kick another child. Polly replied, "I didn't kick anyone, Mum, the game was they could kick me, but I couldn't kick back".

Later that night when her mum bathed Polly she removed her school cardigan and found her white shirt covered in muddy boot marks. Heartbroken she took the shirt into the school the next day and explained everything to the headteacher. Polly was then given supervision in the playground to keep her safe.

Why didn't the schoolgirls tell the truth? Because it would get them in trouble.

Why didn't Polly explain to the teacher? Because this was the first time she had anyone to "play with" and she wanted to be liked.

What would have happened if her mum hadn't seen the muddy boot marks on Polly's shirt? Polly would have been viewed as the ringleader not the scapegoat.

Let's move on to the secondary school years.

Autistic girls may struggle with the concept of lying to make sure they don't get in trouble; they may even not try to cover up their mistakes at all.

I've a fond school life memory of a group of us bunking Art class to go and smoke; our art teacher was really young and cool and would be less likely to behead us if we were late. Our group would sneak out and hang about under the college bike sheds or the local underpass that led to Bracknell town centre. On one such sunny day we had chosen the underpass, when along came the super cool art teacher, hands on hips. The rest of the group whispered a few expletives and quickly threw their smoking materials in the bin, I didn't and gave the art teacher a welcoming wave, smoking gear still in situ between my mouth and a (now much more concerned) pal's mouth, resulting in the group descending into hysterical laughter when Sir shouted "Carly Jones, I know a blow back when I see one" (of course he did he was a cool hippy art teacher).

I couldn't reply immediately to his observation and kind personal disclosure, obviously, as was I mid blow back. But when I had finished and had been marched back to class, I explained that I wasn't inhaling, simply giving what had been requested by a pal, so was not entirely at fault. I didn't try to lie.

He didn't tell the headteacher (thank God) and although he did appreciate my transparency I was, from that day on, viewed as the cocky ringleader of the underpass smoking gang rather than the hanger-on desperate to fit in. I think my attempt at a graffiti tag is still in the subway now, and was at least as crap as my attempt to fit in. Oh well, at least I did some art that day.

More recently, Autistic teen girls have come to me after being accused of shoplifting. By accused I mean that they were set up by their mates, who invited them shopping but put the stolen goods in their bag. And when they got caught these "mates" did a runner, leaving the Autistic girl in serious trouble.

Lola is simply misunderstood as a troublemaker because of her communication differences.

Lola finds the best way to vent her frustrations in the school day is to take a football and kick it against a brick wall in lunch break.

She does this most days. One lunch break a group of teens lean against the wall to chat. "Move or I'll hit you!" Lola shouts.

What Lola means is: "I'm worried my ball will hurt you, can you move please?" The teens don't view it that way, thinking Lola wants to punch them, and so they pick a fight with Lola.

Teachers arrive to break up the situation. If you didn't know the context and the literal use of language used by Lola, who is Autistic, who would you believe? Who started it?

I see it in family court settings too: how easy it is for the other party in the case to set up Autistic girls and women to fail. For example, medical notes with misdiagnosed mental health conditions from an Autistic girl's adolescence can be raked up when they are 40 and trying to leave an abusive spouse and not have their children torn from them.

Past relationships are often informally and formally used to gauge a woman's character. Be that by a new partner assessing the situation before committing, or (more importantly) by family courts and the like. So how do we judge a woman who is trying to leave a toxic and abusive marriage when her track record shows this isn't a one-off? In fact, almost every relationship she's had since her teens has been either toxic or abusive.

Perhaps she is judged as one of those women who like a bad boy, or one of those women who are unable to parent their child safely as they constantly have bad relationships? After all, she's the one who's been the common denominator in all these relationships.

Perhaps we should also see Autistic women's dating history as a sign of their vulnerability and resilience. That "I'm a mug" sticker on their heads that Daisy described has now been re-written to "I'm easy prey" in the adult world. You still can't see it, though.

Domestic violence, gaslighting, coercive control, financial

abuse and cuckooing all rely on the same formula. (Please see Chapter 2 for definitions of these terms.)

1. A partner who has an underlying agenda to control, lie to and gain from another.

and:

2. A partner who struggles to spot lies, may want a partner to give them structure, has an open and honest heart and wants to give to them what they can.

Autistic women, I'd argue, are almost always number two in this formula. So, what is really being judged here? Is it her character or her condition?

If someone was unable to read a foreign language and her actions and words were translated to set her up time and time again, would her character be to blame? Or the translators with an agenda? The common denominator, or the common scapegoat?

STRATEGIES AND TIPS

Having discreet supervision at unstructured time in the playground for the primary school years, discreet student support for the secondary school years and funded non-medical assistance through the university years is imperative for Autistic girls.

This helps Autistic girls access education in a safe and supportive environment without being ostracized by their peers, or creating infantilism in the secondary, college and university years, where independence is a right too.

I cannot recommend Carol Gray's "cartoon strip conversations" more highly.[30] Gray uses cartoon strip scenarios to help an Autistic person navigate, in a social situation, what one person may be thinking (thought bubble) and what they are saying (speech bubble) and seeing if the intended message carries across.

After learning about Carol Gray's cartoon strip conversations, and recognizing that many of the Autistic teens I support are misunderstood in text communications, I drew some stick men (let's face it, they were not going to be good drawings after missing so many art classes). I added a thought bubble above the stick men's heads and a phone screen in the stick men's hands. We then discussed what the stick men might be writing and what they might be thinking, thus supporting the Autistic girl to navigate text and social media communications. It's had great results. Please do check out Carol Gray's cartoon strip conversations for ideas.

As professionals we need to play detective often and keep an eye out for Autistic girls: are they masking more than normal? Has her accent and appearance changed suddenly too? If she has been out of school, this needs chasing up, and if a deterioration in her own happiness or studies correlates to a new group of friends or a new relationship, this may need non-judgemental support too.

Training about Autism in legal settings

It's important that any professional working in the legal system, in whatever capacity, has had Autism training. Not an hour here or there, but regular updated training. Seek out advice from the National Autistic society's website, where they can signpost to the most up-to-date training courses. Expert witnesses in legal proceedings should, if possible, be Autism professionals able to discuss the differences between mental health and Autism.

If a girl seems constantly to be the ringleader, regardless of which group of friends she is with, seek expert advice. Before you think perpetrator, think vulnerable, she may well be Autistic and undiagnosed.

Burnout

Jodie couldn't attend school. It started as playing truant the odd day a week, then progressed into complete school refusal. Jodie's parents became annoyed that she was either deeply unhappy at school and refusing to spend time with or talk to her family, or she was out of school and at home all day doing nothing but scroll through her phone, listen to music and stare at the ceiling – yet would suddenly have a miraculous recovery when her friend asked her to go out after the school day had ended.

Jodie wasn't lazy, selfish or rebellious. Jodie was Autistic. The only way she could have any chance of experiencing the social aspect of adolescence was to have plenty of time alone in a controlled sensory environment with no demands placed on her, no expectation to talk. Naturally she had to continue school and was labelled as a rebel, meaning even more of a parental and professional spotlight was shone on her. This led to a feeling that she was being watched and demands that she keep up with what was expected of an average teen. But Jodie wasn't an average teen. Trying to keep up with her friends while at school meant she was masking more than ever before, not resting or processing emotion- or sensory-wise. Her grades dropped, her friends got sick of her letting them down at the last minute, her friends' parents banned them hanging out with (someone they assumed was) a lazy troublemaker. Jodie shut down and burned out and eventually became catatonic and was hospitalized.

We hear much about meltdowns as a visible sign that an Autistic person is in need of help. In a small Autistic child this is often misunderstood as a "tantrum" and as an adult it is misunderstood as aggression, mood instability or attention-seeking behaviour. It's anything but. It's a consequence of extreme overwhelm brought about by reaching a limit of social, environmental or sensory bombardment.

A meltdown is more likely to be seen in campaign advertising or Autism-related training. Shutdowns get much less exposure and therefore much less understanding from the non-Autistic community. It is known, however, that many Autistic people shut down rather than melt down.

Meltdowns and shutdowns are painful not just emotionally but physically too; it hurts. It REALLY hurts.

Imagine the worst migraine you've ever experienced and multiply that by 10. Head feels as if your brain is mince in a hot pan; eyes feel swollen; every sensory input is affected. Taste becomes numb; the wrong clothing can become unbearable where previously it was annoying; smell feels much like, for the mothers amongst us, trying to empty a cat litter tray when you have the most severe morning sickness. We become less aware of where we belong in space, retreating to an area of safety and stillness, be it a bed, a favourite chair or the spare room at a family member's house. Sounds become torture. Shutdowns are scary. No matter how many shutdowns you experience you are never prepared for the next one, particularly when they hit you with a new ferocity. They feel never-ending and you are left voiceless and unable to move, wondering if this is the shutdown you won't recover from. We do recover, though at its worst it can feel like fighting for your life in a silent battle where your only opponent is yourself.

If meltdown is the visible flare in what feels like being lost in the ocean at night, shutdown is silently drowning.

No outward cry for help, no high octane "explosion", rather an implosion of self, an often verbal and expressive Autistic turning almost mute and unable to advocate for themselves at the very time they need support the most. It feels like drowning but in some unknown sea that only a handful of lifeguards and navy ships have any knowledge of. A flare here, a call for help, would be a useless waste of your last resources and your last chance of being able to swim again.

For me, it feels like tuning out of the frequency that every human is automatically tuned into every morning, tuning in without any agency whatsoever to a higher frequency that only some can hear. I find comfort in our family's assistance dog in these times. I have a wonderful memory of being a small child walking in the vast fields still found in urban Reading with my grandfather's black Labrador, Daisy. Granddad was deaf but gave me a small silver dog whistle, saying that humans can't hear it, only dogs can. I blew the whistle to get the dog to recall and I heard the whistle, which I found funny as I assumed Granddad had spent good money on a normal whistle and been somewhat conned due to the fact he was deaf. I know now that I could simply tune into Daisy the dog's frequency. Now, when the shutdowns start, I can tune into the comforting and mostly nonverbal world of my own dog, Hunter, and I don't feel scared anymore.

It starts for me with everyone sounding very far away, but I can't stay with them, however hard I try (and I try so very hard). This is followed by everyone sounding under water. Sounds from far away feel suffocated and sounds from nearby seem muted.

Then the pain starts, head in a vice, face dropping, speech slurred or non-existent. The context of words is absolutely shattered. Due to this looking a lot like a stroke, I can recall my mum telling me she was worried, and she was going to call an ambulance. I remember just lying there, eyes wide open, managing a tiny nod but not remembering what the word ambulance meant. When they arrived my mum explained I am Autistic and had become nonverbal. They were fabulous and did stroke tests on me in bed, during which I could not even sit up without being pulled up. I had so much I wanted to tell them about my shutdown and that it would end, but all I needed was to get out of pain. I rose to my feet to try to find my way back to the frequency where people talk so I could ask for strong pain relief, but I projectile vomited immediately when I opened my mouth. Thankfully, without a word, the paramedics saw I had reached my threshold and took me to hospital for stronger pain relief and monitoring. I was released home four hours later, fully verbal, without pain but sore as though I had been kicked in the head a few weeks ago, shaking the hands and eloquently thanking the NHS staff who had been so gracious and non-judgmental.

This isn't always the case, however. Often, as previously mentioned, a shutdown is misunderstood, misdiagnosed and wrongly medicated as something else. Many Autistic women I support who can't communicate their diagnosis to paramedics in a crisis are taken to mental health hospitals or have social services investigations after being seen in shutdown.

It's unlike depression: it has causation, and it has a non-medicated ending. It can last hours, days or weeks, but it does end.

It's unlike a seizure, but feels much like one. It differs however as it's not caused by one strobe light, but is a consequence of many "bright lights" over an extended period of time.

It's unlike dissociative disorders, but often diagnosed as such by non-Autistic mental health professionals who haven't experienced a shutdown. Although we may have, at the time of shutdown, limited access to the social information file of others' names, faces and roles, we know who we are, where we are, and we know we want this to end. Dissociative disorders are there as a form of self-protection for victims of abuse and trauma. Although many Autistic people have experienced abuse and trauma, a shutdown will have likely occurred many times throughout their life – even before any abuse occurred. I have heard from parents who, in hindsight, realized the reason their later-diagnosed Autistic children "blanked out" or slept at every birthday party or family event was not down to coincidence. It was due to overwhelm. The teens who tried to fit in with their peers at after school clubs, residential trips or parties at the weekend, and who were unable to bounce back to school on Monday, staying in their rooms so as to not cave in completely. Seen then, this was marked down as lazy or school-avoiding. Seen now, it's a desperate and unavoidable cry for help.

It's also likely caused by masking our social communication differences to the point where you have NOTHING left to give.

It's caused by trying to survive and flourish in a world that really isn't set up for your brain, be that school lighting, post-work social commitments, or the expectation to be at every family event and be on top form.

Without speaking up about shutdowns, we risk misunderstanding and making the agonizing experience worse, leading to an extended shutdown – which may in turn lead to complete burnout and even Autistic catatonia.

Catatonia

"Tell me about your sleep patterns, Carly", my doctor kindly asked, likely noticing that my eyes had that type of sparkle in them which to the untrained eye may appear attractive, but to a doctor with decades of clinical experience looks a lot like someone living on autopilot.

"I'm not a big sleeper, sometimes I have horrid nights and days where I can't sleep at all. My eyes are open and I can see and hear everything around me, but my entire body is in paralysis, I can't even blink." I have a nervous giggle at this point thinking my doctor probably assumes I've really lost it. "I remember one such night where I was paralysed, and my cat was lying on my stomach and all I could think was how terrible it would be if there was a fire, and I could see it happening but couldn't move to save my cat... I used to think I was dreaming but one time I could hear my neighbours having guests over and discussing the table decorations, so the next day I knocked on their door to check they had that conversation. They had, I wasn't dreaming, I was actually paralysed."

"Carly, have you heard of catatonia?" my doctor asked.

I replied "Oh yes, that Welsh pop band I love them!" My doctor, being Welsh, joined in with a smile. "Yes, they are a Welsh pop band, but it's also a medical term for what you experienced when you can't move."

And that's how I found out that without preventative measures, stress management and support, I can stop being able to move. I never got a chance to explain the context of my odd questioning to my neighbours – they moved house quickly after that.

STRATEGIES AND TIPS

There is a three-pronged approach to supporting a young person experiencing shutdown, which leads to burnout, which can sometimes but not always lead to catatonia.

Change of lifestyle

- If we think about Jodie and her struggle to keep up with the demands of life both educationally and socially, what could have been done differently? Were reasonable adjustments made for her in her school? Was she able to have sensory breaks and processing time in the school day? Could she have been given flexi-schooling where she had a limited timetable and was able to have days off or days where she worked from home?

- Could she have had the understanding with her parents, teachers and friends that being Autistic meant this was her normal?

- Can you begin to imagine how distressing and isolating it feels for every day to consist of some sort of overwhelming pain, yet being viewed as lazy, reclusive and an all-round bad egg rebel, when in fact you are in great physical pain?

Prevention

Spotting the signs that the Autistic girl you support is heading towards burnout can in some cases prevent burnout.

- Are they spending more time alone in their room at home?

- Are they more sensitive to sound and light than normal?

- Do their clothes suddenly feel intolerable to wear rather than uncomfortable?

Autistic girls have sensory issues every day of their lives, but when they become stressed it's like sensory issues on steroids.

- Are they controlling their eating more than normal or suddenly have a much more restricted diet in comparison to their normal dietary needs? (More of this under eating disorders.)

- Are they going silent more than normal?

If so, it's time to reassure, ease demands and provide support. Not a time to try to make them keep up with the social norms of adolescence, in peer groups or in education.

Support

Should burnout occur anyway, it may in more extreme cases lead to catatonia. Catatonia is a serious condition which needs professional medical support. As a non-medical professional, this isn't something I should comment on, but I recommend the work of Dr Shah for those seeking more information.[31]

CHAPTER 4

Tried-and-Tested Strategies for Support

Working with individuals

Laura was 15 but far taller than me and looked much older than her age. She had her own office attached to the classroom at her school with her own computer, a bean bag and a door that accessed the green area if she needed a break. I was told that Laura didn't engage with others and didn't talk. I was also told she wasn't happy to have a new visitor and likely wouldn't take in any of the safeguarding lesson, but they wanted to try.

I entered the office to meet Laura and she gave very little eye contact – a relief, I don't like eye contact either. I got a chair and asked to sit next to her as she watched a cartoon-type game on her computer, a game designed for someone much younger than Laura, maybe a toddler. Laura has a learning disability as well as being Autistic. I watched her for a while and remarked on how I liked the colours of the characters. She gave me a smile then opened up a webpage on her computer and typed away quickly on her laptop and the colours on screen changed. "How did you do that?!" I asked. Laura smirked and giggled with pride pointing to the coding box on her PC. "Laura can you teach me to code please?" I asked, absolutely elated about just how brilliantly intelligent this young Autistic girl with "learning disabilities" was.

She showed me how to code and manipulate PC controls on videos and websites. I told her she was one of the most intelligent 15-year-olds I'd ever met and shared that I knew how it felt to be underestimated and that I was sure she must feel frustrated and underestimated every day.

Laura immediately stopped showing me how to code and quickly reached for the dry wipe pen in my bag and started almost stabbing me with the black felt tip pen all over my face. Laura's support worker said if at any point I wanted to leave I should. I don't know why, but I wanted to stay; I didn't think Laura's aim was to hurt me, I thought she was communicating.

Laura then stabbed the felt tip pen into my hand about 25 times, she paused (thank God, she was really strong) then Laura drew around the pen dot-to-dot in my hand. As she connected the dots it was clear she had drawn hearts on me.

My heart imploded.

We didn't get through many safeguarding sheets that afternoon, but I hope knowing someone saw her brilliance, and knowing that someone else knew how underestimated she could be, gave her a self-esteem boost, which is the foundation of all safeguarding anyway.

This was one of those days at work that will be carved in my memory forever. Both because I'd seen the most brilliant ability and talent in someone described as learning disabled and also because I had to do the food shop at ASDA after work with black felt tip dots and love hearts all over my face and hands.

The four Ts

I suspect the subject of working with individuals could be a book in itself. However, as an Autistic professional working with and for Autistic girls, I have found that considering the four Ts keeps me on track. They don't just help me as an Autistic individual, they also help make my work accessible for the Autistic girls and their families.

It may be that a non-Autistic professional using the four Ts won't find them as easy to engage with, and it may take some time to employ these strategies automatically. If this is you, that's OK. Even as an Autistic professional I sometimes forget too; all that matters is that you correct things when you remember. You may already use the four Ts without realizing or there may be a work policy or code of conduct that uses some of these strategies. Some may feel unorthodox for your particular line of work. If only one of two of the four Ts helps or is appropriate, that's OK too.

Three of the four Ts – Timekeeping, Text communication and Terminology – are the most frequently needed for accessibility and to avoid causing offence or a misunderstanding with the Autistic girls you are working for. The fourth T, Telling tales, is needed far less than the others as it is highly dependent on the context. I have added it however, as it has had good results in terms of safeguarding young Autistic women, particularly when intervention is needed more urgently.

TIMEKEEPING

Be on time. In fact, in performing arts if you are on time, you're actually very late. You have to be on location to prepare, and then you'll be on time.

If you are awaiting an appointment with an Autistic girl and her family be there 30 minutes beforehand. It's likely she will want to be early too. If you can't be early or even on time due to unforeseen circumstances make sure you communicate this to the Autistic girl's family as soon as humanly possible.

TEXT COMMUNICATION

Written instructions and rules in advance can be very helpful.

Language matters. I remember one Autistic girl being taken swimming with her friends and told: "Do not jump in the deep end or talk to strangers." Her parent then spotted her jumping in the deep end, and talking to a stranger. The request was perceived as: "If you jump in the deep end, you'll have to talk to strangers," rather than: "Please don't jump in the deep end and remember also to not talk to strangers".

Text or visuals can help with rules and safeguarding requests.

When it comes to older Autistic girls with their own email accounts, accessible emails matter! Emails are often full of "fluff" pleasantries, stock sentences about the weather or latest national news and then the dates, deadlines, duties and requests get lost in a sea of words.

This best way to formulate an email could look like this:

Good morning [name],

I hope you are well. [Write short sentences.]

I am emailing you to let you know what we will discuss at the next college council meeting.

Subjects will be:

- *Use of sports hall*

- *End of year party*

- *Leaving photos. [Use bullet points.]*

*Can I ask you to email me back with suggestions you have about the above subjects **by 15th May,** please? [Be clear about what you want someone to do and when you want them to do this by.]*

Thank you!

Kindest,
Carly [Use Arial size 12 as it's easy to read]

It is really important not to say "look forward to seeing you next Wednesday!" Why? Because what does NEXT WEDNESDAY mean to you? If it's Sunday, does next Wednesday mean in three days' time? That's the NEXT Wednesday. Or does it mean Wednesday NEXT week, so not the next Wednesday at all?

Dates and times should be explicit, e.g., May 15th, 2022 at 20:30 hours. Not "Next Wednesday at 8:30", because this means the Autistic guest could travel a week early and also be there for an 8:30am breakfast and not 8:30pm in the evening!

Even at 38 I struggle with this. It's made me early for an interview by a week, early for a catch up with far away friends by a week, and is even to blame for the fact I ended up divorced at 25. Had I not turned up a week early to a dancing job at 18, I wouldn't have been on stage at the exact same time the only attractive male on the rota was – my ex-husband.

I therefore cannot begin to stress how VITAL communication of time management is.

TERMINOLOGY

Think about the terminology around Autism you are using as a professional.

The language we use to talk about Autism is important because it can affect how Autistic people are perceived. Talk about Autism in a balanced and matter of fact way to the Autistic girls you support. There are many wonderful things about being Autistic, and that means many Autistic girls will be proud of the fact they are Autistic. They will see Autism as part of who they are, rather than something separate, and prefer to be described as "Autistic" rather than as "someone with Autism".

I am often left baffled by the phrase "she lives with Autism". If that's what I'm doing, it's about time Mr Autism started paying towards the household bills: what a sponger.

Even worse is the phrase "touched by Autism". Blinking heck.

Don't refer to an Autistic girl as having symptoms of Autism. Symptoms are for the common cold: preventable, catchable and curable. Autism is not preventable, catchable or curable.

Don't say she is suffering from Autism, she isn't. She is only suffering from you assuming she is suffering.

TELLING TALES

Not in a telling-a-lie sense, in a literal telling a tale, telling a story sense. Often in my one-to-one work with Autistic girls if they feel unable to vocalize or start a conversation in the appointment I will initiate a conversation by being the talker rather than bombarding them with questions that often aren't answered. This requires careful management, however, as it's HER appointment time not MY appointment time. So how to navigate this?

Before the appointment time or within the appointment time, strike up a conversation informally, discussing a TV show, book, film or news event that touches on a situation similar to the one the Autistic girl is experiencing.

For example, if I knew an Autistic girl was drinking a lot to impress her boyfriend and I knew from previous conversations that the boyfriend had once sadly lost a cousin to drink driving, I would speak about a news event/TV show/book or film with similar themes (in this case, I might describe how a character broke up with their partner as they were teetotal after losing a family member to drink driving, while their partner liked to drink a lot down the pub). It's not necessary to use a real story, it's just a prompt to start conversation, and is often far more useful and has better results than drawing a social story for older Autistic girls – who are slightly more mature and likely at that age to perceive drawing a social story as patronizing.

Working with other professionals and agencies

You may be reading this as a non-Autistic professional or an Autistic professional who supports Autistic girls. Some suggestions will be for the benefit of Autistic professionals supporting Autistic girls, but my hope is that it helps non-Autistic professionals to consider their own vulnerability and practice in a universal way too.

The four Rs!

The four Rs, much like the four Ts, are the four strategies I have found most useful to remember when working with other professionals and agencies. Not all will help all the time, the context being dependent on your profession and the other agency or professional you are working with at any one time. However, Relationship, Research, Recommend and Remember would all be good starting points for an unwritten code of conduct to be used by professionals supporting Autistic girls. If we engage with these principles then we should ease some of the most difficult situations and be able to work together to deliver a good outcome for the Autistic girls themselves.

RELATIONSHIP

Maintaining a relationship with other professionals is vital to progress safeguarding for Autistic girls. Working together, professionals can help fill in the gaps, see the bigger picture for the Autistic girl they aim to support and make safeguarding happen, faster.

RESEARCH

When working with Autistic girls and their families, decades of hard graft can be undone in minutes if you ally with an organization, charity or individual that is a cause for concern amongst the wider Autistic community. After all, the aim of advocacy is to support the wider Autistic community.

But for all professionals there is a balance to be found in refusing to work with anyone who has made mistakes in the past (and maybe even present?) and joining them with a hope of working from within to make things better. Preaching to the converted, however safe for reputation management, isn't always going to make changes where they need to be.

Research is vital – it won't always mean you say an outright NO to being an ally or working with an organization, charity or professional. It will mean however that you need to ensure that your capacity there has an independent nature and that you know when to leave if it's a fruitless endeavour. If, as a professional yourself, you are also Autistic, it may take an additional mental health toll. I have the utmost respect for Autistic professionals, particularly academics who spend year upon year researching their chosen niche of Autism, having day and night to read and digest materials with terminology and intentions that are personally offensive. There is no greater example of resilience and dedication than an Autistic professional who has gained their undergraduate degree, Masters or PhD in a subject matter that affects them personally, in my opinion.

Saying "No, thank you" to a hefty sum of cash if you are self-employed is never an easy task, particularly if funds are low, there's a mortgage to pay and mouths to feed. The reality is, however, that this can very often mean having to do just that. If the affiliation is with a project that would likely do more harm than good, morally you have to decline. I've been offered daft amounts of money in the past to team up with the medical model "cure" multi-billion-pound machines around Autism. Did I need the money? So much. Did it make me sick to look in my dependants' eyes and refuse the cash (not literally we all would have hated the eye contact)? Yes, I may have almost vomited with guilt several times.

We can't sell out though – it matters too much.

Plus, we can't be cured, nor would we want to be, so it was a laughable and anger-inducing proposal in that sense.

I know of advocates for various causes who have turned down offers of cash to stop speaking out, cash that would have been enough to buy them several houses outright and ensure they never had to work again, being able to focus entirely on their caring duties. They refused. Big salute to you if you're reading this.

When you politely decline however, you may still make the situation better for others in doing so.

I won't mention names as the company I am about to use as a case study is doing much better now, and also, I don't want to get sued (although it's true!).

Many years ago, I was invited to keynote for a company who wanted to highlight how vital Autistic employment was, how they valued Autistic people and how they remunerated Autistic people accordingly.

What a breath of fresh air! Although the keynote would take an eight-hour round trip on a train, meaning I couldn't work the day before or after and would have to organize childcare, I said yes as I wanted to support the company.

That's when it got sticky.

I asked what the speaker fee was – there was none. It was assumed that the Autistic speaker would keynote for free. Not ideal if you have offices, expenses and insurances to pay each month but I'm still happy to do a few volunteer gigs a year if it will have a wider ripple effect for others. I wouldn't be out of pocket, just wouldn't gain anything personally.

Sadly, the cost of the train trip, running to several hundred pounds, would also not be covered.

So, a company that wanted to demonstrate to the UK that they valued Autistic workers by having an Autistic keynote were happy to allow the Autistic professional to give up three days of work, speak for free and also be several hundred pounds out of pocket.

Ironic.

I replied politely explaining that the set up wasn't actually doing what it said on the tin and I couldn't stand up there and praise their company for an hour or more when that wasn't an authentic representation.

I can't lie. The rebel inside me was highly tempted to go anyway and then stand up on stage and tell the truth. It would have been devilish fun, but it wasn't worth me forking a few hundred quid out for the hour of joy that would bring, and also who are the audience going to believe? Me on my own as an individual, or a massive company who would likely play my honesty down by referencing my condition: "She's disabled after all!", "Probably needs a break", "Oh is this lack of empathy?" "Ahh, so THAT'S a meltdown!". You can hear it in your head before even turning up.

Also, I have a duty to ensure that when I represent Autistic people, I leave a good impression. Consider this if you are also the first openly out Autistic professional the audience are likely to meet. My concern was that, if I made a "stand", I'd make matters worse for all. So, I just sent the polite decline.

A few days later, another advocate messaged me to say they were the keynote for this gig: train paid, even got a fee. I was delighted. Seriously chuffed. Sometimes the best work you can do is saying no. But always say why, in a non-judgmental manner, politely if you can (have a cuppa first if you need it).

Now imagine you were the CEO, events manager or employee of a brand, company, organization, body or charity that, without proper research, unwittingly allied with a company who behaves like this? (I should probably say behaved, as I said, that particular company is doing things much better now.)

Many Autistic people know that the company has a reputation among the community for treating their Autistic workers like a token add-on, ferried in one day a year to make the company look good to their funders and partners. If you walked in the Autistic person's shoes, would you want to work with the company now?

Research comes from asking the community you aim to serve directly before big choices and partnerships are made. Social media may be your best friend on this one. Before signing up to ally with another professional/company/project you can simply search Twitter by using a hashtag in the search bar, reading up to gain a perspective, or even better run an anonymous online survey asking the Autistic community for feedback more generally on the companies they have had good or negative experiences with.

RECOMMEND

With the aim of connecting with people and services that are ethical, recommendations are also needed. Not just for yourself as a professional, but for your fellow professionals!

Genuine recommendations help the Autistic girls' families find support that is effective, well tried and tested and reasonably priced. It helps them find it fast, time being of the essence here. As I stated in the Introduction: "Autistic girls find themselves in vulnerable situations that keep happening like clockwork, day by day, month by month, year by year. A race against time for them all in a timeless systematic flow chart."

If we aim to support the safeguarding of Autistic girls, we need to share good practice often. This means that the family won't waste time and send limited financial resources in the wrong direction.

REMEMBER

Remember that just as you may be supporting an Autistic girl who has come to you after her diagnosis and you are in the process of ensuring she doesn't experience abuse and negative life experiences, you may also be supporting Autistic girls who are coming to you from the other direction. They have already experienced the abuses and negative life experiences, but not yet had their Autism diagnosis – they may not even be aware themselves yet.

If your profession works in or with:

- eating disorder clinics
- children taken into local authority care
- children excluded from school
- youths who have attempted suicide or who self-harm
- young offenders
- county lines
- homeless hostels
- teenage mum and baby hostels

you may well have Autistic girls in your care. Look out for them.

Remember a diagnosis is a privilege not an expectation.

Remember that according to the Equality Act 2010, accessibility is needs-led, not diagnosis-led.

Keeping an intersectional mindset

In recent years, intersectionality has become a fashionable buzz word in diversity and inclusion spaces and on social media platforms. The concept of intersectionality itself, however, is far from recent; the term was coined in 1989 by Professor Kimberlé Williams Crenshaw.[32] Intersectionality considers various forms of discrimination including race, gender, sex, class and so on. How does intersectionality affect Autistic people?

Diagnostic overshadowing

Until fairly recently it was considered unlikely that a child with Down syndrome could also be Autistic. We know now that this is of course possible, and as a consequence more Autistic people with Down syndrome have a dual diagnosis. However, having a physical disability can often leave Autistic people without their Autism diagnosis.

I'd say 9 out of 10 parents of Autistic children I have worked with have told me their Autistic child was tested for hearing difficulties before their Autism diagnosis. Why? Because sometimes parents and professionals can assume an Autistic child's developmental and communication differences are due to a hearing issue. It seems that professionals will often refer an Autistic child to have their hearing tested as a means of eliminating this as a cause of the difference. It is only when the test shows no hearing problems that Autism is discussed.

So, what if the Autistic child happens to be deaf too? They are sent to have their hearing tested and when the test shows that they are in fact deaf, then the Autistic traits and potential diagnostic referral is abandoned – leaving the deaf and Autistic child with support for only one of their two disabilities. An interesting finding is that: "Autism is at least 10 times as common among blind people as it is among the general population [...]. And children with autism may also be more likely to have vision problems than typical children."[33] This is a pattern that's been noticed in the Autistic community for years.

Diagnostic overshadowing means that many people with a primary disability are never diagnosed as Autistic as every challenge is viewed as being due to the primary disability; but there's far more to it and more Autistic people are out there without the right neurodivergent support and understanding.

Intersectionality has practical consequences. For example, as advocates, educators and safeguards, we can't always rely on visual aids for Autistic visual thinkers who cannot see well. What about them? What about this intersection, within an intersection?

We know that historically Autistic girls have faced clinical misogyny, and that this continues today. It has traditionally been believed that Autism affects males and females at the ratio 3:1.[34] Many UK Autism professionals believe the truer statistics to be 2:1, possibly even 1:1.

Levels of awareness within the general population about gender and Autism are improving. You can tell awareness is improving when it evolves and almost folds in upon itself. In recent decades, we have moved away from "Only boys are Autistic!" to "Hey girls are Autistic too!" to "Wait a minute, why is Autism gender specific at all?" Which, as a long-standing advocate for Autistic women and girls, pleases me. The role of an advocate is to put your entire life into a cause with the sole hope that you will one day make your campaign null and void, because the growth in awareness has over time delivered equality. In Chapter 1, in the section "Team diagnosed vs. team undiagnosed", when discussing how many diagnostic tools have historically left Autistic girls behind, I can't help but also be thankful that the very tools that left Autistic girls un-diagnosed did, at least, exist. I wonder whether it was by campaigning against the male-based models of diagnosis, which were developed to find Autistic men without learning disabilities, that Autistic women and girls without learning disabilities came together and found each other? I am concerned that wider awareness of how sexuality, race, culture and socio-economic background intersect with Autism is not improving at the same speed as awareness of Autistic girls (yet!) and it is my sincere personal and professional wish that this changes fast in order to safeguard as many Autistic people as possible.

How do we safeguard Autistic girls when their intersections make diagnosis even harder to obtain?

Learning disability

When Annie first contacted me I received an email that was about four pages long. I know emails don't have pages as such but if I was to print it out it, my guess is it would have run to around four A4 pages.

Annie's use of the English language was exquisite. Words I have never heard in my life. Don't get me wrong, I adore the English language. With Annie's email however, I felt like I needed a thesaurus in order to do it justice. It was an eloquent, intelligent and brilliantly constructed email.

At the end of the email, Annie gave me a telephone number. She wrote beside it: "Please only ever text me, don't call this number. I can't answer it because I'm nonverbal. I'm in my 30s now but I've never spoken."

I was blown away. I started to ponder what everyday life looked like for Annie. I wondered if she was diagnosed in a timely way as Autistic, or if she was diagnosed with a learning disability, even though her ability was clear for all to see in her email. Does she experience people talking about her in front of her but not including her? Does she have a PA and support system?

I wanted to question my own unconscious bias too. If I'd just met Annie, would I have ever thought that she was this eloquent? I know that sounds awful. I'm so glad I got that email, because it's really helped shaped everything work related I've done since. It's helped me understand that just because somebody can't talk, or chooses not to, it doesn't mean they have nothing to say. And just because someone can and does talk, it doesn't mean that they always know a lot.

Gender

In the Introduction to this book, I had to make promises. I promised that focusing solely on girls should not be taken to mean that I do not understand that Autistic boys and men need safeguarding too. They do, particularly if they face healthcare and legal proceedings, or if they have learning disabilities or other disabilities which have resulted in their Autistic diagnosis and support not happening as they should have done. And this is where I need to expand on that.

In the context of this book, my area of knowledge is better served by focusing on Autistic girls. Autistic women and girls are who I've worked for and with for 13 plus years in advocacy and I can bring personal insights to the role.

More importantly, I have huge admiration for the male advocates and parents of Autistic sons who campaign for their rights, who relay their own sometimes horrendous accounts of a life misunderstood and their own vulnerabilities that can only come from first-hand lived experience. For me to write a book about safeguarding Autistic boys would tread on their toes; it's also their book to write, not mine.

I feel I would also do a vast injustice to Autistic boys to write a 60,000 word book that, frankly, they could write much better. Same goes for the gender fluid, LGBTQ+ Autistic community – their unique perspectives mean it's their story to tell.

With that being said, as professionals we also cannot overlook the gender issue clouding diagnosis. What about the ever-blurred line between gender-based diagnosis expectations and stereotypes? I fear that, as with any pattern, there will still be a group within the Autistic community that will be indirectly excluded from early diagnosis and support. That somewhere in the midst of the mass explosion of "female" traits of Autism, Autistic males who present with more stereotypically "female" traits will not fit neatly into either camp, and so be left without diagnosis and support. This will result in a pocket of the Autistic community again subjected to a pattern of vulnerability, health implications and lack of resources. I feel as an Autistic female, who experienced first-hand the consequence of missed or misdiagnosis, that I have a duty to try in a small way to ensure these experiences will not repeat for Autistic males who present with more stereotypically female Autistic traits.

Someone who came to me through my advocacy work

validated my thought process about the complex relationship between gender and equality of diagnosis. The contact came from a father – heterosexual, happily married with an adult Autistic son. This man contacted me to say how similar we seemed to be to one another. He had Autistic traits but was not sure he should be diagnosed as Autistic. He self-identified as having primarily a male brain with some female tendencies. He believed that all the ambiguities in his profile would make it very difficult for him to get a definitive diagnosis. I thank him for the courage to write to me which in turn gave me the courage to write a published paper titled "Gender fluidity prism in diagnosis of autism", which was based on a survey in July 2015.[35]

My survey indicated that males are as much in need of gender neutral diagnosis and safeguarding as females.

Some of the qualitative feedback surprised me.

I (present) more female, when I finally worked it out it was because I realized I had heightened empathy and then discovered the intense world theory, empathy is thought of as being stronger in females. (Non-diagnosed Autistic male with Autistic family members)

Gender identity should be included in diagnosis rather than being a separate thing, it's all about education of the people who diagnose. Gender identity is something not all healthcare professionals understand at a care level. (Diagnosed Autistic, gender neutral)

I am more relaxed and contented in the presence of female company as opposed to male company. (Diagnosed Autistic male)

I feel I'm somewhere between female and A gender, I certainly don't feel fully female. (Diagnosed Autistic female)

[Stereotypes of Autism] should be more fluid given the number of Autistics who are gender dysmorphic. (Male, awaiting diagnosis with Autistic son)

I am more interested in stereotypical male interests. (Diagnosed Autistic female)

My interests include complementary therapies and New Age spirituality and I find there are many more women interested in these things than men. I am not interested in sport, cars or typical male pursuits. (Diagnosed Autistic male)

Person centred diagnosis which is tailored to the person [...] meeting a person with a blank slate [...] I am gender fluid so that does have an effect on my views and experiences. (Diagnosed Autistic person)

I had not thought of male Aspies exhibiting more typically feminine Aspie traits, but it does seem logically possible. (Diagnosed Autistic male)

Sexuality, gender and neurological diagnosis are all separate elements yet utterly at the core of one's being, identity and a part of what makes us who we are. They therefore affect how we present. It is vital to understand all the elements that make up a person in order to understand them and their traits in practice.

Are our rigid stereotypes of both gender and Autism preventing us from seeing a bigger picture? And does this mean that there is a bigger pool of individuals who are lacking diagnosis and so lacking support?

After being contacted by males who identified as being Autistic but were without diagnosis, this complexity became clear. One male had visited his GP and been turned away as he was not thought to "look" Autistic, as can so often be the case for females. This male is homosexual, and perhaps this was a hurdle as stereotypical, outdated, rigid expectations around how a homosexual male presents may have caused clinical confusion and therefore medical exclusion. Could it be that the gender of an Autistic person is very different, not only in its presentation but also in its nature, to that of an individual who is not Autistic? If our very nature is different, can we apply non-Autistic gender roles in a carbon copy fashion to Autistic experiences?

Gender, of course, is not simply a matter of nature; our gender is also a social construction and is fluid, not fixed. So, over time, and over the lifespan an Autistic person's gender roles (and so their Autistic presentation) can change. In both timely and late diagnosis, this should be taken into account to promote inclusion.

Autism is often referred to as a spectrum, and there is also a spectrum of gender. When relying on black and white thinking, statistics and quantitative research, human experience is often number-crunched into figures, which feel safe and reliable yet miss out a wealth of information about the human experience, where the pattern of human behaviour is all too often replaced with the pattern of numbers.

A long-term focus would be to ensure all clinicians have been trained in gender neutral tools and how to interpret the answers to questions to be gender neutral in semi-structured interviews.

Whilst big data is vital, so too are qualitative voices, where the patterns of behaviour can really be heard and understood. How a professional diagnoses and supports an Autistic person in semi-structured interviews is much like a prism, a reflection of the understanding, knowledge and experience of the clinician who diagnoses. The Autism spectrum is vast and beautifully complex. Some individuals are easily identified as being Autistic and given a swift diagnosis, support and their human rights. However, for many individuals the triad of impairments, which clinicians historically referred to as the essence of Autism, remain transparent until the appropriately trained clinician shines their knowledge and their light onto it. It is only then that the colours and complexity of the prism can be seen and understood.

In the tsunami of awareness around Autistic girls, professionals must also seek out and safeguard the forgotten boys and men.

Ethnic minorities

The Autism diagnosis process in the UK has for many years been saturated in stigma, myths and a degree of misogyny – Autism once being considered a very "male and pale" condition.

The first hurdle for ethnic minority individuals is often being able to receive an Autism diagnosis in the first place. This is by no means down to racist behaviour, but due to diagnosis, gender and cultural complexity. Autism is often neither considered nor recognized in girls or women, and this is especially true for ethnic minority females.

In 2016, via an informal survey posted on social media, I asked ethnic minority Autistic women about their experiences.[36] A great deal has changed since 2016 as Autism is a fast-paced world; however, the feedback is still worth noting:

- 85% felt they were not reflected in media

- 50% felt that Autism was viewed more as a "white condition"

- 100% felt there were far fewer ethnic minority Autistic women at support groups than they expected

- 87% felt that ethnic minority Autistic women were left out of the discussions around women and late adult Autism diagnosis.

Where does this leave ethnic minority Autistic girls?

In recent years, due to the hard work and efforts of charities, the media and individuals, there has been long-awaited progress in awareness of ethnic minority Autistics. This is not yet universal, there are still areas – particularly areas with greater racial diversity – where diagnosis and support of Autistic females is difficult to obtain. In my professional experience, in the UK, the Midlands in particular are struggling to protect their Autistic women and girls as swiftly as other areas.

Many non-Autistic ethnic minority professionals have

shown reluctance to diagnosis Autistic women and girls from an ethnic minority background. Sometimes this is due to lack of awareness, often it is due to a clinical fear of making the ethnic minority Autistic woman more vulnerable with a label – this is viewed as a double discrimination, rather than the vital protective measure that it is.

With the above in mind, protecting ethnic minority Autistic women and girls from abuse and sexual violence is a many-layered issue.

Many Midlands-based Asian women travel to Berkshire and London to gain support from Autism advocates for their Autism diagnosis and to gain protection from further abusive relationships.

All Autistic individuals have the human right to meaningful, timely diagnosis and support and diagnosis should be a right rather than a lottery.

Working with the families
Working with parents: The three Bs:
Boundaries, Believe, Balance
BOUNDARIES

There are many professionals to whom Autistic girls' parents will look for support, but we'll focus on two main avenues here:

- Authorities and educational professionals

- Volunteers and low or unpaid advocacy they find online.

You may imagine it is easier to have professional boundaries if you fall within the first category, but that is not always the case. Why is that?

Well, often parents to Autistic girls are Autistic themselves. Although Autistic adults are generally very polite and respect-ful, they are still Autistic! They are often misunderstood and ruffle the feathers of authority figures as they may not react to hierarchy in the way that a professional expects given their (the professional's) position.

It is really important not to perceive this as a lack of respect or even as rebellion from the Autistic parent. Hierarchy is a social construct, Autistic people of all ages are arguably less socially constructed and therefore not going to play the game of hierarchy as well as you'd expect. This in no way makes an Autistic parent rude. Imagine not understanding hierarchy? What could that look like?

Cindy is an Autistic parent. She had a day to herself and went high street shopping and noticed a homeless man had food and was searching the bins. Cindy went into the supermarket and bought him a huge lunch and took it over. She then sat eating lunch with him, chatting away like old friends.

Why? Well, obviously, she felt worried about him not having any food but also because she found chatting to him as enjoyable and normal as she would chatting with anyone. She doesn't see hierarchy.

What do you think of Cindy? Kind? Selfless? Good, because she is!

Cindy however is also the parent that the schoolteachers, police and social services assume is rude, problematic and defensive. Why? Because she talks to them in exactly the same way she talks to anyone, with open honesty and humour, like an old friend. This confuses the life out of professionals who think she is either:

- up to something

- hiding something

- rude and or unprofessional

- not taking the matter seriously; irreverent.

Same parent, same style of communication, differently perceived due to the context of the situation.

It's important professionals know an Autistic adult is Autistic. And it's important to know that a parent of an Autistic girl may well be Autistic themselves.

What could a misunderstanding of hierarchy look like with authority figures? I'll give my own face-palm experience to spare someone else's experience here.

I recall late one Sunday afternoon driving to pick my eldest daughter up from the cinema and noticing there was a blue light of a police car behind me. Obviously, I knew I wasn't doing anything wrong, I was driving slowly and I wasn't wanted by the police for a major crime so assumed it was meant for someone else and carried on driving. The blue light continued, I was too worried to turn around and see who they were after as I wanted to be driving the best I could, but I felt awful for the officers struggling to get to whoever they were trying to flag down. When we stopped at the traffic lights, I even looked at the officers and smiled with a "hope you get them" shrug.

The police officer didn't smile back so I carried on driving in a sensible fashion and pulled into the cinema car park.

The police car, with blue lights and sirens still blaring followed me into the cinema car park; I was really panicking now as I was worried that something awful had happened at the cinema and my daughter was there without me.

As the officer and I got out of our cars I asked him what's going on, probably in an unnatural way as in my mind I was worrying about my daughter and whether there had been a crime at the cinema.

He was pretty mad at this point: "Why on earth didn't you stop for the blue light three miles ago?"

"Oh, was that for me? Blimey!" I laughed, probably with relief that my daughter was OK and as I was genuinely baffled.

"It's no laughing matter! What do you think I am pulling you over for?" he asked.

"Speeding?" I replied (first thing I could think of?!).

Now he's really mad. "Are you trying to be funny with me? You were driving at 28 miles an hour in a 40 miles an hour road!"

"So not speeding then?" I asked, smiling.

"I think you know why I'm pulling you over."

I didn't.

"Have you had a drink today?" he asked, making full eye contact – ouch.

"No, of course not I would never drink and drive". Now I'm super offended. I despise drink drivers.

The officer made me take a breath test in front of my daughter and her mates (awkward!), but a test which of course came back showing that I had absolutely zero alcohol in my system.

"I am amazed that came back clear, you had all the traits of a drink driver, driving with window open, below speed limit, sitting too close to steering wheel then not pulling over", he explained.

I replied "That's just how I drive. I don't want to break the speed limit rules, or any rules. I even indicate in empty car parks just in case. I'm not drunk, I'm Autistic". This is probably where I should have stopped but my unfiltered honesty kicked in and I was powerless to stop it. "But actually officer, I was also surprised that test came back clear too as it was my birthday yesterday and my family and I had quite a bit of wine this time 24 hours ago and even after a day you'd expect there to be some wouldn't you? That's why I waited to drive until later today." I was smiling at him to try to make this all better, trying to let him know it was OK to get it wrong, no hard feelings my end, that type of thing.

He wasn't impressed and drove off, I took my daughter home and pondered over what I could have done differently. Pondered what type of parent and driver he must have thought I was, pondered if other professionals have wrongly perceived me and my parenting in the past, pondered what unwritten boundary I had crossed and what expectations of authority's boundaries he had that I didn't live up to. I was incredibly sad about this for days. I still, years later, have no idea why the way I communicated with him had made him so angry. I have many family members and friends who are police officers, I respect them, the law and the rules so very much, but somehow I had made him think the complete opposite of me, my parenting and my actions and it hurt. It still does, if I think about it.

Many professionals refer parents they consider troublesome to me – be it parents in legal proceedings, parents in EHCP meetings, parents in school appeals and more. I try to help both parties understand one another – not through expert knowledge, just because I learn well by making mistakes.

Let's think about how professionals who aren't uniformed authority figures who are working as volunteers or advocates may struggle to keep their professional boundaries when working with parents – Autistic parents, or indeed non-Autistic parents – too.

Social media
Social media is a fabulous marketing tool and way for professionals to connect with parents seeking their services but also a fabulous way at blurring the boundary lines from the outset. After all, one social media site declares all connections "friends", so there we have it, where is the boundary for the professional? Ideas about how to navigate this are in the "strategies and tips" below.

Phone numbers

It goes without saying that it's vital to obtain a phone that is solely used for work purposes if the professional needs/wants or is bound by professional standards to keep the relationship solely professional. If the professional is both a friend and supporting an Autistic girl's parents with their professional services, that's a different matter.

BACKGROUND

Not all parents of Autistic girls are also Autistic. Some are, some aren't, some are but haven't been diagnosed, some are but have no idea they are. But I find the best way to tackle that is to assume all parents who come to me needing support or advice for their Autistic girl are Autistic. Because that way I make sure that support is not just accessible for the daughter but accessible for the parents too.

If parents aren't Autistic the accessibility support won't affect them. I think of it like entering a building. If you are planning a building but only have the budget for either a) stairs or b) a ramp, my hunch would be to build the ramp. If the guest uses a wheelchair or has a baby in a pram, the stairs are going to be an issue. If you have a ramp, you won't prevent those able to use stairs accessing your building, but you'll also make it possible for those who need a ramp too.

Considering a parent's background is important. All of us as human beings are layered creations! Our childhood, our DNA, our disabilities, the cultural context or the religious beliefs we are raised in mould us into what we see as typical and what we see as different. It also means for professionals supporting an Autistic girl, the better we relate to and take time to learn about the parent's perspective, the better we can help them support their Autistic daughter and ultimately work together as a respectful parent–professional team.

BELIEVE

When, as a parent, you feel misunderstood by the entire world, just hearing someone say, "It's OK, I believe you" can unlock a door and drop guards. Parents of Autistic girls are often not believed.

In the Introduction I said someone can only be an expert if another personal calls them an expert, they can't just self-declare it. So, you know I mean it when I say this: parents of Autistic youths are the expert on their child.

They may not be the expert of a whole field of scientific research, had 10 years of clinical experience or attended Cambridge, Oxford or Harvard and, yes, they may sometimes drop their daughter off to school whilst driving in their PJs, but about this one Autistic girl they are the expert.

The parents' insights, wishes and suggestions for their child must be balanced and respected in healthcare settings, because they have seen their child in their own environment, at their best and at their most vulnerable. They have seen the patterns of behaviour, the likes, the dislikes. They know what can cause them distress and pain because they have spent 24 hours a day 7 days a week for many years doing everything they can to keep them safe and happy.

Parents of Autistic girls face extreme challenges when planning how their household needs to be run in order to be able to best protect the mental health and happiness of their Autistic daughter. If their Autistic daughter also has demand avoidance traits/diagnosis this is tenfold. Parents are often put into a difficult position of judging what they can share with professionals in order to be believed and gain support for their daughter, and the natural parental responsibility for safeguarding their daughter's right to privacy.

Let's give an example of this.

Shayla is 12. She has sensory processing issues, is Autistic and has started her periods.

The sensory side of her periods became so bad that she was unable to leave her room, let alone her house to attend school once a month. The GP decided to put Shayla on a contraceptive pill to stop her periods as her daily life became unbearable: if she wasn't having her period, she was worrying about having her period.

Three months after taking her pill, having no bleeding whatsoever, getting her life and education back on track, she was due to attend a school trip but had a breakthrough bleed. She was not now having a period but was, frankly, hysterical. This period wasn't expected, it came out of the blue. Sensory issues were now at boiling point; Shalya could not leave her room, let alone attend the school trip.

Shayla was disappointed, in sensory pain, tears, and too humiliated to have ANYONE know why she couldn't go to the school trip last minute, as all her non-Autistic class friends could cope. She begs her mother to not tell anyone why and make up an excuse, a headache for example.

So, what does her mum do? What would you do?

a. Ignore your daughter's pleas for privacy and tell the teachers and her friends the truth? Your daughter will be mortified, but people will understand just how challenging it is to be the responsible parent who gets their child to school on time.

b. Respect your daughter's right to privacy, call the school and parents of friends and pass on the message as requested by your daughter that she has a headache.

Obviously the problem with B is that it only works once. If you have a headache or any excuse each month, people may start to reject your daughter, assuming she can't be relied upon to turn up. The invites stop. Teachers start viewing the parent as irresponsible, dysfunctional, disorganized, too soft...

But parents will still often choose answer B, because while telling the truth to friends, family members, and even having a vent on social media to find some solidarity on SEN forums would give the parent a virtual hug, it would be at the expense of their daughter's embarrassment. So they just don't choose option A – ever.

Parents of Autistic girls and indeed the girls themselves shouldn't HAVE to reveal the most personal and private experiences, vulnerability, and private care needs to be believed. I know that with diagnosis as much information as possible is advantageous, but professionals who aren't diagnosing and are supporting an already diagnosed Autistic girl should believe and respect the clinical diagnosis rather than question, judge or undermine it. At all times professionals should give space and respect to both the parents and the Autistic girl they support in their private lives.

BALANCE

When transparency is not just advantageous but legally required, professionals need to find a balance between the duty to provide privacy and the duty to fact-find and undertake the legal job at hand. Balance comes with a duty to make sure that, when making these judgments, accessible questions are employed as standard.

Let's think about the court and child protection professionals here. I have supported Autistic parents of Autistic girls in social services, family court and legal issues in my advocacy role. I'm not legally qualified. My main purpose is to provide support, and to ensure that any Autistic-specific misunderstandings in either language, communication, social imagination, literal understandings or jargon are clarified between the parties to promote an accessible hearing. As I am not a trained lawyer, I cannot make any warranties or representations of any kind with regards to legal advice or suggestions. I am simply in place to help support and share any Autism-specific needs in court cases.

Autistic parents often contact me at a time when they are extremely distressed and in need of some support. The natural reactions that these cases bring for anyone going through them are unfortunately felt all the more by Autistic parents – the life-changing uncertainty leads to additional stress and trauma-related health issues.

Autistic parents in legal proceedings are extremely anxious that they will let others down and be reprimanded due to their Autistic communication style. In turn this leads to additional stress-related fatigue which leaves them unable to prepare a "court bundle" in time for hearings.

In the past Autistic parents have told me how scared they are that they will be thrown out of the court room and not listened to or understood. Autistic parents may have their reactions and responses easily misunderstood in a court situation and therefore require clarity of language and instructions, and time to process information and time to respond to answers.

Lucy was one such mum. When she was asked by a judge: "You attended the parenting course as suggested, what did you get out of it?" she replied, "I got so much out of it, in fact I met another Autistic mum, and we are going to meet up for a drink next week."

This was written down as "Mother cannot put her child's needs before her own." Maybe, IF she understood the context and the implications of the question, but she didn't. Lucy replied honestly and literally. "What did SHE get out of it" was the question.

Had the judge asked, "So Lucy, you've been on the parenting course as suggested. What parenting strategies did you learn to help your parenting in the future?" Lucy would have reeled off 101 strategies she had learned and how they would help her child. But she wasn't asked that, was she?

Lucy didn't get the outcome she should have had and sadly passed away soon after. A heart-breaking miscommunication. Made even more stinging by the vitally needed Cambridge study of Autistic women's experience of motherhood later published, which concluded: "There was no difference between Autistic and non-Autistic mother's ability to prioritise their child's needs before their own."[37]

As an advocate this haunts me daily. Although there were many factors that led to this, I can't help but blame myself when a parent I have aimed to support passes away. It's also a reason I have continued to write this book despite some events being extremely painful to recall. Because if there comes a day when I do not feel I can continue to work in parental advocacy for the sake of my own wellbeing, at least there will be a book out there to signpost professionals to.

Time and time again I am asked to help translate the questions and add context to court proceedings. Often though, when an Autistic parent asks for an accessible hearing and an Autism-trained court intermediator, they are simply offered "Easy Read" materials and left to it. Easy Read has its uses, yes, but it's the context, consequence and construction of questions that we need to work on, not just bigger font and photos.

Many Autistic people have executive functioning issues and have a great deal of difficulty being able to complete forms and be aware of impending timescales and deadlines. This, with any additional health issues on top, can sadly mean that work/favours/tasks they've agreed to do whilst trying to be helpful can become overwhelming and last minute.

Autistic parents of Autistic girls will need those in court, in all roles, to show them disability understanding, care and compassion at an incredibly anxious and uncertain time.

I believe this to be not only a disability issue, but a human right to a fair hearing.

STRATEGIES AND TIPS
Boundaries

If as a professional you use social media as a marketing tool, it's wise to have a business page and social media accounts that are solely for business where you and other team or staff members have access to private messages.

If you are a sole trader with a small turnover and no staff, you can add to your bio that all business enquires should go to your email address and not be via direct message. It's a hard one to do but you will have to either ignore any messages that don't respect your boundaries or, if a business request is sent to you by direct message on a social media platform you use personally, send a stock reply message: "Please email me; this is a personal account".

It helps set a boundary not just for them, but also for you. I had to get very serious about professional boundaries when I was being called on my phone at 3am by complete strangers whom I had connected with on social media.

It's imperative.

If you are struggling with your email inbox and wanting to reply to as many people as possible to ensure they feel heard, you will exhaust yourself. An out of office automated reply is helpful here. Mine says I'll reply to as many emails as possible within three to five working days and also includes a helpline text service number so those in critical need have been signposted.

It is much harder not to blur the lines between working and friendship when a volunteer worker. Friendships are, of course, a wonderful result of meeting new people and can be navigated successfully alongside a working relationship. But for those of you who wish to maintain a separate working/support/volunteer relationship, you have to have strict boundaries in even the most informal of settings. Strategies to navigate this include keeping conversations (be that talking or text) solely about the Autistic girl you are supporting. Do not weave personal issues into the conversation. If for example a dad of an Autistic girl you support suddenly wants to talk about how you can help his business or how you should do lunch, you can try replies such as "I am at full capacity for business consultancy at the moment but have an opening in three months, and my hourly rate is…"

Referring to the lunch invitation specifically: "That's a kind offer, thank you, but I use much of my free time volunteering and need to save time for my own family/friends/dog!" If they continue to pester, you will just have to say sorry not interested, block them and ask for a different family member to bring the Autistic girl you support to see you in future. Be kind to yourself on that one!

Believe

Professionals who have no safeguarding concerns should offer a codeword for parents to use if they want to respect their daughter's privacy when asked questions. For example, the school could set "dental appointment" as Mum's code to say, "she cannot make it in today; she is safe and well but I can't disclose why". This saves the receptionist and whoever is hovering around the school reception at that time hearing it all.

Professionals with authority, such as the police, social services and the like should all have regularly updated Autism training. User-led training which gives real life examples of how to understand all Autistic adults, including Autistic parents. In the court system, training for legal professionals and intermediaries on how to work with Autistic parents is vital for the chance of a fair hearing. Especially in family law.

Balance

Setting your expectations out at the first visit can help before any discussion has taken place.

- What your role and responsibilities are

    Let them know your job title, how you will manage things in the meeting (especially if you know them from a different setting), explain how reporting safeguarding concerns is part of your duty, letting them know you will not discuss what they say (unless it's a safeguarding issue) and if you don't know them from another setting do let them know you will not wave or say hello in the street as their confidentiality matters to you.

- What their role and your expectations are

    That they are here as a parent (even if they happen to also work in fields related to their Autistic daughter's needs) and all conversation is about the Autistic daughter with a view to making things better for her, discussion of any other nature has to be made via a separate consultation meeting.

- Accessible email and date formats

    Many parents of Autistic girls are also Autistic so make sure you don't misjudge them if they are late or early or don't show up. This may not be because they don't care. Check:

    » Have you used accessible emails and dates to arrange the appointment?

    » Have you sent a reminder text?

The life-saving gift of a peer group

The first time I met an Autistic female (knowingly), I was in my 30s. That's if we don't include my Autistic daughter (then I would have been 20).

It seems a bit of a sad state of affairs if the only chance of feeling less alone in this world and meeting another human being remotely like you is something that can only be achieved by cloning yourself. Before we get diverted by that thought, I want you to think about your own uniqueness and what makes YOU you? Do you have blue eyes? Long dark hair? Brown eyes? Olive skin? Do you have a thick accent? A beard? Do you have dyslexia? Are you gay? Do you have a physical disability? Are you very tall? Maybe you have a hidden disability? Maybe the language you speak is misunderstood by a lot of people?

Now try to imagine a life where you're a teen and so far, you have been told other people with blue eyes/dark hair/brown eyes/olive skin/a thick accent/a beard/who are gay/who have a physical disability/who have a hidden disability/who speak your language exist – but you've never actually met one. Imagine one step further: you've never even seen another person like you, because although people say they exist and that there are loads of them, you haven't seen one on TV before either.

This lack of anchoring and lack of a tribe on top of being misinterpreted, misunderstood and in many cases mistreated day in day out; this isolation of not knowing where you fit in the world has, from what I've seen, a more devastating emotional impact than any of the other challenges faced by Autistic girls.

You scour history books and schoolbooks to find one other person like you and there's not much there.

The same happens for Autistic girls' self-identity. Without self-identity, how can they create self-esteem? Without self-identity leading to self-esteem, they can't cultivate self-confidence and self-protection.

Spending time with other Autistic women for me, an adult, feels like I've been walking around in high heels all day and

I can finally slip my fluffy slippers on. If I make mistakes in my language, prefer to text rather than talk, explain the day's frustration and excitement by info dumping, I'm met without judgement or misunderstanding.

I'd never considered myself a possible candidate for having long-term friendships with females. Friends were often older men usually leading to a power imbalance or, as a teen, vulnerability. Or with gay men, where sexual relations didn't have to be navigated. However, what I really needed was another Autistic teen girl to meet and be friends with. It gives Autistic girls a safe, loving and fair chance at female friendship. No agenda, no being misled, no being misunderstood or punished for saying the wrong things, a friend like every other non-Autistic girl seems to get, because they fit in.

It's a very special find to bond with someone who speaks your language. But how can our Autistic girls find their much-needed bonds?

I became very frustrated in my work as, due to privacy reasons, I could not ethically connect one Autistic girl and her family to another young Autistic girl and her family. Day after day, week after week, month after month. I would have, for example, an 11am meeting with a college-aged girl who was being bullied and wanted to take her own life due to loneliness, then at 12:30 I'd have a guest with exactly the same issues. They often lived in the same town but I couldn't grab a note pad and say "Hey, here's the address of a girl who you'd really get on with!" That's a HUGE no in confidentiality, obviously.

I could, however, open the office up for those Autistic girls and their families on a Sunday. They could pop in for a cuppa, cake and a biscuit (trust me there's always cake and biscuits) aware that there would be other Autistic girls and their families there.

So, a few years ago that's what I did. Activities range from arts and crafts, to outdoor games and sport if the weather's good, I set up photo booths for them, make soaps or slime – all very average things, but it's them being together and the way they interact, care, accept, support and understand one another which makes it far from average. Once a year, I am fortunate enough to take this small group of Autistic girls to the Commonwealth Day celebrations at Westminster Abbey with the Queen and many members of the Royal Family in attendance.

I can't begin to explain the impact this had on the girls. One of the girls had come to my office a year before worried that she wouldn't have any friends to spend her birthday with the next year. She later joined the Sunday club and made friends; the beautiful irony was that by complete coincidence her birthday landed on that particular year's Commonwealth Day service, so she actually need not have worried at all. She spent her birthday with a group of established friends and also the Queen – girl power!

Not all the Autistic girls who attend Sunday Club joined because they visit me for an advocacy appointment, sometimes they're simply Autistic girls who are home educated or don't have other Autistic girlfriends at school. Sometimes it's parents who gain the support from other parents. For some girls it will likely be the only time they are with other Autistic girls, or indeed the only time they socialize at all. Although, sadly, all at some point had issues with isolation and lack of a peer group, the change in the girls' lives from what I've seen and from what their parents have fed back has simply been unprecedented.

STRATEGIES AND TIPS

- You don't need to make "Autism" the reason for the club.

- Safeguarding is important. If you are in a professional safeguarding role always undertake updated training for continuing professional development, you'll be surprised what you learn.

CHAPTER 5

Designing and Sustaining a New Blueprint

The untapped oil source

Time for blue sky thinking that I hope in no way glamorizes being Autistic but, having spoken about the huge vulnerability and challenges that Autistic girls face, it's only fair to talk about their strengths as well.

I truly believe that Autistic people of all genders are an untapped oil source. Not just for a country's economic development, but most importantly for their own happiness and their own personal experience of life.

What if we tip-toed or dived into what could have been, and make it what will be? What if an Autistic girl's life, diagnosed or self-identified, was supported from the very earliest opportunity? The world's ultimate empathizers; the world's greatest asset, hidden in plain sight, finally seen, valued and understood.

The unique, yet at times predicable, flow chart of patterns of strengths utilized and recognized as acutely as our support needs. The fixers of the world, be that in the technology, science, engineering or academic sense.

The social fabric fixers, the foster parents, the vets, the charity workers, the civil servants, the advocates, the policy-makers, the animal welfare campaigners, the climate change experts, the cyber security and secret services chameleons, the mums, the teachers, the police officers, the lawyers, the artists, the dancers, musicians, actors and poets.

Seeing and experiencing the world in a bespoke way which in turn helps the wider world see something beautiful and meaningful, and gives purpose and direction in times when solutions are desperately needed. Imagine a world with more of that richness in every corner of society?

Autistic women living their happiest and most fulfilled lives, instead of being snuffed out too soon by child sexual abuse, bullying, discrimination, suicide, eating disorders, domestic violence, unequal access to healthcare, homelessness and unequal justice systems.

Imagine it, now, and whatever professional capacity you are reading this in, think to yourself: what one strategy can I use today to start to make this happen?

Ideas for the education system

Nicole loves art; she only wanted to paint, draw, sculpt and create her way through school. As her long-term aim is to be an artist, she struggled to find any motivation whatsoever for traditional lessons such as maths and English, often refusing to participate in these subjects at all. Her mother heard about the launch of an art exhibition where the artist was an Autistic woman. Nicole's mum decided to take her to the launch. The artist kindly answered any questions the guests had. Nicole asked if it was fun being able to paint all the time as a job. The artist replied candidly saying that sadly only 20 per cent of her working week was actually painting. Eighty per cent of her time was working out budgets, writing to sponsors and paying her exhibition staff, so maths and English were incredibly important to be a successful artist too. Following this exhibition visit Nicole had motivation to keep her English and maths lessons going to a good standard; it was now logical. Nicole knew she needed these lessons in order to be an artist.

Valuing interests and favourite subjects as the foundation for topic-based learning would be a far more useful way to engage an Autistic girl than nagging and punishing her because she has lost motivation for traditional subjects.

In fact, most school-based subjects can be found within a student's favourite topic. Despite assumed rigidity of thinking, there is actually real flexibility inside an Autistic person's special interest!

Let's say the Autistic girl's interest is horses:

- Maths could mean budgeting for the horse's food, hay, stable and vet's bills. Perhaps if the horse takes part in show jumping, angles could be taught.

- English could be writing a newspaper article on the horse's latest outing.

- Geography could be looking at the different breeds of horses, where that breed originated from and what different grounds and natural habitats those horses experience.

- History could be looking into the treatment of horses, how they were more commonly used as transport before cars and how animal rights have changed throughout the years.

There are many great educational subjects to be found in topic-based learning, if Autistic girls are taken an interest in, understood and planned for. Think about an Autistic student you know: how could their favourite topics help them access traditional subjects?

The school building itself can be challenging from a sensory perspective, as well as socially exhausting and painful. Ideally, just as workplaces are changing into more sensory-friendly environments, our schools should be too. In the meantime, just as we offer flexible working for adults as standard, we should also be offering flexible schooling as standard, without years of appeals and a mental health crisis for the Autistic girl first.

In 2020, the educational world changed forever when almost all students were sent home to access learning online. (For parents of Autistic girls who cannot access mainstream school, they were already home educated so not much changed.) Can the education system learn lessons from the coronavirus crisis? Could mainstream school settings be more flexible in their thinking about what a school week looks like? Could Autistic girls completely out of mainstream school be invited to join a school at a pace that is accessible for them?

Maybe attending on a Monday to get the materials and goals for the week, learning from the accessible home from Tuesday to Thursday, watching the classes online, and then attending school again in person on a Friday to hand in the week's work and have time to reconnect with her friends? This could mean gaining GCSEs in an inclusive and accessible way, without being excluded, burned out and falling out of education entirely.

Let's think about the GCSEs and exams in general. An example of an implicit English exam question would be reading an article from a newspaper about the local authorities removing a 100-year-old tree to make a new road, then being asked,

> "In the article we read about Grant, talk about how Grant feels about the tree."

Right, that doesn't make much sense. Questions need the context: who, what, when.

- Who is Grant?

- What is his connection to the tree?

- When are we describing his feelings about the tree? When it was on his land? When it was being cut down? Or now, two years after it's been removed?

So, exam questions are often a test in themselves, before the Autistic girl has even begun to write her answer. Why not ask the exam question explicitly?

"In the newspaper article Grant who owns the land the tree was on had spoken about how the tree had been in his family for many generations. How do you think Grant could feel seeing the tree being cut down?"

Much better.

But why are students expected to take up to 11 GCSEs in one academic year at the tender age of 15 or 16? As an adult would you ever decide to take 11 online courses or exams in one summer? What would be the effect on your happiness and mental health? Now imagine you are also Autistic and trying to navigate the teen years too. I don't understand why we continue to do this to young people (all young people not just Autistic girls) when in reality they only need four or five great GCSEs to get into college.

Mental health must come before grades, always.

Of course, many of these comments are really aimed at Government and policy makers, rather than individual educators in the classroom, where the focus has to be on implementing the latest requirements in the most effective way possible. For those teachers amongst us, I'd say thank you for all you do. Please try to be flexible and open-minded as you think of ways to deliver the curriculum – your support and understanding can make all the difference to our Autistic girls.

Finally, though, a word about the phrase and misconception about someone being "slow". The injustice of how this word is sometimes thrown about in relation to Autism really bothers me.

It bothers me as an advocate, it bothers me as an Autistic woman and it bothers me mostly as it's a huge misunderstanding. Autistic students aren't slow, they are overwhelmed.

To the onlookers, yes, a student may need extra time; they may need the right environment to complete a task set for them and may seem to require more time to do what their peers are doing. But they aren't just doing what they're peers are doing, they are doing so much more.

They are slow to process the single instruction given as they aren't just processing that single instruction. They are in fact processing every original idea and every thought and memory related to that instruction as well as the external environment at that time.

In my early and mostly unsuccessful university years, our class was taught about the bottleneck theory. We were asked to think about the drive to university that day. To think about the route taken. Then asked how many blue cars did we see? How many people walked past the road we drove on etc?

Then we were reassured that of course we wouldn't know how many blue cars or how many people we saw as the bottleneck of our processing wouldn't allow for that. We were able to ignore the masses of information from our eyes, brains and memory bank, only thinking about and remembering the drive itself.

I didn't know I was Autistic then but felt this was false information as not only could I recall the drive itself, I could also recall the elderly lady who was walking on the side of the road with a Jack Russell wearing a pink collar. I could recall the number plates of the car in front of me in the traffic and laughing at how it made a word. A particular favourite rush hour pastime of mine was to give cars names based upon the registration plates and what the mixture of numbers and letters sound like when said out loud.

It would appear that I don't possess this bottleneck that most humans do. So maybe that's why I drive slowly and with more caution? Not because I'm slow but because an everyday task can overwhelm me?

Think about the Autistic students in class listening to the teacher's instruction to, for example, write a paragraph about Victorian Britain. The guess is the student would be expected to write a concise paragraph based on the factual information given by the teacher in the presentation beforehand. The date, the type of clothes, the monarch of that time. But, what if your memory bank held more?

What if, simply by hearing the word Victorian, your mind, without the aid of Google, kicked into internet search mode and you are thinking of workhouses, which leads you to think of the work of Charles Dickens, which pings up another brain search from the memory archives of Oliver Twist, that in turn reminds you of Easter Sunday and being able to watch the film on TV with your family. You start thinking about technology and wonder if Victorians had televisions and if they didn't what did they do for entertainment? That in turn ignites a memory of Punch and Judy shows at the seaside and you start to wonder what ships and means of transport were available in that era? If they'd been alive in Victorian times, what would they have invented to help aid progress?

The rest of the class has written a paragraph which summarizes (copies down) what the teacher has just said. The Autistic student still has not said a word, they still haven't written a word and to the onlooker they are perceived as struggling. The Autistic student staring into thin air or at the wall or out the window isn't slow. They are super-processing.

They are not only listening to the teacher's knowledge, they are listening to their own knowledge. They are not only learning second-hand information, they are creating first-hand ideas.

Imagine you have a video you want to upload to YouTube. You have two laptops to upload this on and want to see which laptop uploads the video the fastest.

Laptop A is uploading the video at the same time as having

32 other tabs open, less battery left and is also uploading all other videos that relate to the subject matter. Laptop B is only uploading the one short video asked, has no other tabs open, has a full battery and isn't wired to automatically upload any other video which relates to the subject matter. Laptop B will upload the video faster, but does that make it more advanced? A better choice of engineering for all forms of job roles and employment?

Laptop A takes longer to upload the one video and needs to have the charger plugged in so it doesn't shut down mid task. Does that make the laptop inferior? Does it make the laptop less efficient in all forms of job roles and employment? Does that make the laptop slow? Or is the laptop doing more and is just temporarily overwhelmed?

Ideas for employment and media
Media

In my advocacy work I strive hard to ensure that the voices and insights shared are not solely personal. There's a big difference between self-advocacy and professional advocacy and although our own lived experience can help systems become more user-led, it doesn't aid consultancy on a broader level as it's too specific.

Grassroots work is therefore vital for Autistic advocates who want to evolve from self-advocacy to professional advocacy. How can we amplify the voices of Autistic girls living as young girls in today's world if we don't listen first-hand to what is happening?

Sadly, one of the most common pieces of feedback I have heard from the Autistic girls I support is that the word "Autistic" is used as a derogatory term by many non-Autistic teens. Be that online, in the school playground or within friendship groups. Way back in the 80s and 90s I overheard kids saying, "You spastic", "Are you blind?", "Are you deaf or something?" Times have thankfully moved on from these heart-breaking insults, unfortunately I've been informed that now, when a young person does something their peers consider stupid it's, "Are you Autistic?", or "That's SO Autistic". So how can we expect a recently diagnosed Autistic girl to be out and proud about her neurodivergency when the term itself is the pinnacle of "not cool"?

Role models are vital for Autistic girls and for their peers. They help to safeguard their ability to "come out" as Autistic and safeguard their mental health and self-esteem within the school system. There should be well-consulted representation of what Autistic girls are and aren't in all aspects of media. The subject of diagnosis is much less scary if girls can strike up a discussion about Autistic roles models which her peers may find cool: footballers, quiz masters, popstars, artists, scientists, social media stars etc. The more non-Autistic teen girls feel comfortable with, understand and respect Autistic people in general, the more an Autistic teen girl will feel comfortable with, understand and respect herself, which is the foundation to her safeguarding.

STRATEGIES AND TIPS

- Ensure your media-based organization has disability role models and creates ways to ensure accessibility for performers with disabilities to gain roles.

In 2017 I was fortunate enough to be chosen as one of the 32 BBC Class Actors for the BBC Class Act scheme. This was an initiative run by the BBC to provide a residential training and support package for disabled actors to increase the representation of disabled actors in media.

I wasn't the only Autistic actor present, there were a few Autistic women and Autistic men and also many actors with a vast range of disabilities, be that they used a wheelchair, had visual or hearing impairments, learning disabilities, had been born with physical differences or had lost the use of limbs as an adult. This was a real learning curve for me that heralded the start of my journey not just back into acting, but into pan-disability advocacy.

Why? Because I learned that the importance of representation isn't just about those with hidden disabilities being seen. Representation of those with physical disabilities may have been visible but often in a "caricature-ish" way. Those with loss of limbs were often cast as injured soldiers, shark attack victims, robots with ultra-modern arms and legs. Others were often assigned bit parts in TV shows, where they were in an accident and ended up in a wheelchair.

Why could they not be cast as a primetime, full-time actor playing a scientist, who happens to also use a wheelchair? Why not a primetime, full-time Doctor who happens to be deaf? Why not a primetime, full-time lawyer who happens to also be blind? Why not a primetime, full-time, divorced working mum of two who happens to be Autistic?

Yes, disabled actors are absolutely right to feel the frustration of non-disabled actors playing disabled characters when there are so many hugely talented disabled actors out of work; however the frustration also lies deeper.

Disabled actors don't just want to play a role that is a tokenistic brief role, pushed in on a squeaky trolley for a day then squeaked back out when they have played a character whose storyline is solely about their disabilities and nothing else.

Human nature with its vast and beautiful width and breadth deserves authentic representation. Script writers should write characters that have a 360 degree life. So instead of a character who is an Autistic girl, whose whole storyline is about her being Autistic, why not a character who is female and Autistic, but the storyline is about another subject matter completely. Let's say a local crime investigation-type drama – she lives independently, is gay, detests the smell of her police officer wife's cooking, but happens to be the top scoring mum on their kid's PTA evening school quizzes.

Why not an Autistic teen girl character, where the storyline is about a group of teens who meet at a convention each year as they are all popular on social media and have monetized that platform? Why not a storyline that is not just about Autism alone, she enjoys horse riding and photography and has a dual heritage background, her mum is Indian, and her dad is Japanese.

With neurodivergency and Autism becoming more and more high profile and, therefore, also for our younger people, at times, completely misunderstood and with "Autistic" being used as a slang term, it's vital that media take responsibility for consulting professional Autism advocates to review scripts, edit myths and add depth and ensure a layered character is available for the (hopefully Autistic!) actor playing the role before it's aired.

Employment

In light of my lack of GCSEs, I took up an apprenticeship to gain my A level equivalents in a vocational way. The apprenticeship was in a legal company where my main role was to try to look nice, make the tea for the big boss's multimillion pound meetings and when the draft contracts had a grey area (an aspect of the contract that was under dispute) and couldn't be used, I would have the honour of shredding the documents.

I was sacked from this NVQ setting as I completed my qualification early, within five months rather than the two years they were funded to have me, which seemed to displease them. I was told in the board room firing experience by the big boss that she knew she shouldn't have taken a teenage mum on who, in her opinion, was irresponsible for having a baby. "Congratulations on qualifying whilst being homeless and raising a child at 16" would have done instead.

I even bumped into an ex-colleague at the shops year later and they said to me, "The shredding really piled up since you left". Their use of humour, I imagine – but the joke was on them. "Still making loads of mistakes then?!" I quipped back.

It was this legal office however that lit my passion for policy and legal drafts. I'm a fast reader and spot patterns. It was clear how, when you have black and white thinking, you can see the grey area quickly – it's the only part that doesn't make sense, so why's it there? Some 20 years later it's this hidden skill which I use to review medical research papers before they are printed in major publications, assessing the transparency of grant applications for huge amounts of funding before they are green lit, helping fellow Autistic peers and Autistic academic friends debate the contents and reviews of publications used for Parliamentary notes by the House of Commons and House of Lords: policy guidelines for disability Acts, guidelines for national charities and Government department guidelines on safeguarding Autistic youths from child sexual exploitation, radicalisation, gangs, grooming and more.

Lottie's parents were worried that at eight years old she was fascinated by unsolved crimes and murders, and that her favourite book described the mystery of Jack the Ripper. They sought advice and were told to either ban the obsession completely or hope it phased out. The interest didn't phase out, Jack the Ripper street tours around London with grandparents became the treat in lieu of a pink and flowery themed birthday party with friends. This young Autistic girl is now an adult woman training to be a forensic psychologist to profile the UK's most hardened criminals; she is not, I repeat not, a serial killer.

Work is often an Autistic woman's best friend. Our special interests become an employment base. Yet special interests are all too often viewed as obsession or a symptom of their "disorder" akin to a rash that shouldn't be itched as the parents fear it getting out of hand. I disagree. If the special interest is safe, healthy and does no harm to the Autistic girl or others, scratch that blinking itch!

Our interests often become a force so powerful it safeguards us back towards enjoyment and structure in a sometimes cruel and uncertain world. Our interests can also become a foundation to our employment.

Whilst we are here, why are we calling them special interests? If anyone not Autistic had spent year after year dedicated to researching, learning and talking about a specific subject matter, they wouldn't be judged as having an obsession, symptom or special interest. The non-Autistic adult would be an expert. So let's call this obsession, symptom, special interest what it really is: an expertise.

Self-esteem, self-belief and the personal expectations for an Autistic girl start in the home. If her expertise in a subject matter is seen as valuable, and appreciated and welcomed rather than mocked, invalidated and described openly as useless, she will more likely leap into an adulthood where she can thrive rather than suffer in the mainstream.

Work experience, be that voluntary or paid Saturday jobs, can be an enjoyable way to learn the ropes in her chosen area, gaining contacts and industry insights to set her up for life.

Gaining a job in her chosen niche may not be as straightforward as it appears. Often niche workstreams are only available to those who know someone else in that industry, the well connected, the wealthy and it's the old "it's not what you know it's who you know" tale. So how do we promote social mobility for those Autistic girls who have (at least) a triple discrimination: gender, disability and poverty?

JOB INTERVIEWS AND BARRIERS TO EMPLOYMENT

I notice often that feedback on why a job application was unsuccessful is only given if a candidate got to interview. The guaranteed interview scheme means disabled applicants who meet essential criteria are always given an interview, and will, therefore, require feedback if not successful. Could this in fact create a discreet hidden hurdle/loophole for disabled applicants here that isn't being addressed?

After all, if you HAVE to give feedback as to why a disabled applicant is unsuccessful (at interview stage), wouldn't it be easier to just not give them an interview to avoid the awkwardness of being viewed as discriminatory or not PC in that feedback? Isn't it easier to just say "sorry they didn't meet essential criteria" and therefore not be held accountable? This is where strong HR departments and processes are needed to ensure there are robust checks and balances in place to prevent this happening in practice. It would be interesting to compare data about those who disclosed disabilities and those who didn't.

Perhaps it would be useful to both the applicant and the organization to have not only the GIS (guaranteed interview scheme), but also, let's say, a GAFS (conveniently coined term as I was in the process of moving to a new house when I dreamt this idea up – who doesn't love a pun!).

Guaranteed Application Feedback Scheme (GAFS)

If every applicant that is Autistic, and indeed all disabled applicants who declared their neurodivergency/disability, were supported under the GAFS this would mean that feedback had to be given if they made an application. This would help the organization battle any apprehension around drafting awkward feedback, as, interview or not, the feedback would be required.

GAFS could help the organization's data collection, as more disabled/neurodivergent applicants may declare their protected characteristics.

The GAFS could lead to more neurodivergent/disabled/

Autistic applicants gaining an interview; if the feedback that's normally only required for those unsuccessful at interview stage is required for all who declare their disability/neurodivergence, why not get them in for an interview? This would give the candidate a shot at challenging mindsets around what they have to offer: transferable, unique and out of the box insights, perspectives and assets that they may not be able to demonstrate on paper. And even better, transferable, unique and out of the box insights, assets and perspectives that may ultimately lead to new solutions, innovations and progress.

Autistic and disabled people have no choice but to be innovative in their everyday life as life in general isn't set up for their necessities. If necessity is the mother of all innovation; I believe new solutions and country-wide progress is likely the daughter of diversity and disability. We have already discussed the importance of an Autistic girl's interests being valued as expertise rather than obsession. As she becomes an Autistic woman, others need to value this expertise as they would any other professional's work, not constantly see her as an "expert by experience" rather than an expert in her own right.

Knowledge outweighs their confidence

There's that great phrase "his confidence outweighs his knowledge", and confidence and conviction in your actions are a key component of success in the interview room. To have bulletproof board room confidence you have to be either:

a. Extremely aware that your skill, talent and expertise is rare and perhaps yours and yours alone, and be able to sell yourself.

or:

b. Good at vocally communicating and illuminating your work experiences making them seem a bit more substantial than they are – in other words, blagging it a bit.

Unfortunately for Autistic applicants it's often a different experience. Our knowledge usually outweighs our confidence.

Accessibility isn't always as obvious as audio loops, Easy Read, accessible stairs and ramps, and sign language. Sometimes, accessibility is a set of bespoke, discrete measures taken to ensure that an Autistic professional can work without pain or distress in the workplace.

I have to be strategic every day as a working Autistic woman. I dream of being full-time employed, yet my experiences of full-time employment to date haven't made full-time work accessible. I have had to remain self-employed because it means I can be in charge of my accessibility. I don't have one boss, and I am not my own boss; in reality I have many bosses to please. My roles are based in anything from airports to the arts, train stations to TV stations, theatre boards to public boards – they all have one thing in common. The bosses I choose to work for have been trained in Autism and disabilities, are the boss of an Autism and disability-based project or, even better, are disabled themselves.

I can't be the only one who feels that way. That's why having Autistic and disabled employees at all levels matters, you'll increase the likelihood of disabled applicants applying to work at your company if they know you already have a diverse employment base. Because without that ethos of understanding difference and accessibility needs, I know that I simply couldn't work for them long-term and exclusively. I've tried and it isn't sustainable. I don't claim disability benefits for myself, although my daily life is impacted. I chose not to claim, although I understand why others do or may be in a position where they have no choice. Really, I want to work just like everyone else.

This is what frustrates me the most when we hear the statistics around how only 22 per cent of Autistic people are in any type of employment.[38] Frankly, this makes us feel like oxygen thieves and, worse than that, means we have to rely on others to financially support us. But it's important to remember the following:

- It's not the fault of the Autistic community that the workplace our skill set matches hasn't caught up with Autism Accessibility training yet.

- Most of us do want to work and have incredible talents and skills to offer. We just need to work differently and to not be stigmatized or viewed as lazy, difficult or demanding for wanting that accessibility to take place.

- The value of a human has no correlation to their productivity, but to be supported to be able to feel fulfilled and gain independence is not only a great feeling, it's a safeguarding issue too. The more financially independent an Autistic girl is as a woman, the more likely she is to have the means to escape an abusive relationship.

Equality vs. equity, disability vs. diversity
Businesses, organizations and public bodies need to ensure that disability, although a diversity matter in a broader sense, isn't diluted down to diversity boards and schemes.

Diversity is about equality. It's about making sure everyone gets the same opportunity, leading to a fair chance of employment.

Disability is about equity, making sure everyone gets the accessibility support they need in order to have a fair chance of employment.

Imagine this as watching a tennis match. Everyone is given one front row seat: equality. The deaf person still cannot hear the scores. The blind person still cannot see the match and needs two seats for their partner or PA to sit with them. The wheelchair user feels stuck at the front and needs two seat spaces for their chair and another chair for their PA or partner to help them navigate the steps. The Autistic person with an assistance dog would have felt calmer at the back as it's shaded, and the sunlight is giving them sensory overload, and their dog is definitely distracted by those tennis balls.

To be able to have a fair chance of being able to enjoy, and importantly sustain their time at the tennis match they all needed different things, not all the same. For retention of disabled staff, equality won't work, only equity does.

For Autistic people in need of context often Easy Read is handed out. Easy Read presents complex texts in an accessible way, for example with short sentences and clear language.[39] Yes, Easy Read is very helpful and yes, it gives context, but for many Autistic professionals it's not covering their needs and sometimes can be seen as undermining their abilities. It's not that Autistic professionals struggle to take in information, it's often the case that we take in too much information and need someone to bullet point the information needed by being explicit.

So let's say, for example, there is going to be a launch for a new report into offshore energy windmills. An Autistic woman who has had a passion for climate change since she was a girl and now, as a woman, is an expert engineer in her own right will be a panel speaker. The report is sent to her via email six days before she speaks at the launch.

Is she expected to:

a. Read the entire report, search the references in the report, read all the academic papers mentioned then prepare an hour-long PowerPoint presentation talk from childhood climate change interest to her professional offshore energy expertise, giving a time line of how we got to this report?

b. Read the areas of the report that will be covered in the launch and write a five-minute speech about its importance?

c. Read the report in full and just take some notes in case she is asked spontaneous questions during the Q & A?

Easy Read won't help to cover all her concerns here. Easy Read will help her have a visual of the day's agenda, but it won't explain the expectations of her from others, leading to vast anxiety. Remember the:

- Who?
- What?
- When?
- Where?
- How?
- Why?

in the email correspondence in Chapter 4.

Here's an example:

Dear Emma

*On **28th October 2021** [when] we would like to invite you to **Conference Room 2 at the Savoy Hotel** [where] to **be our key-note speaker and talk for an hour about your journey from child climate change campaigner to being a world respected engineer** [how] for the **launch of our report on climate change and offshore energy** [what].*

*The audience will consist of **journalists and CEOs of oil and gas companies** [who].*

*Our aim is to **gain more awareness of the benefits of offshore energy in the news** [why].*

If you'd feel comfortable and have availability to attend, please do email me back with your fees.

Kind Regards
Mr (I own lots of Windmills) Smith

Why do Autistic girls grow up to be great employees, CEOs, civil servants and public office holders?

Autistic women have a natural skill set that can't be taught or bought. Be it a tenacious, blinkered drive; passion for justice and elimination of injustice; focus; time keeping and strategic skills; traits of loyalty or great respect of rules.

I recall one day being emailed the Nolan Principles, the Seven Principles of public life that must be adhered to by those wishing to work in the public interest. I was apprehensive about reading the Nolan Principles. I assumed that this would be the point where I would have to hold my hands up and declare myself useless to the cause of public service as my inability to comprehend hierarchy and my unfiltered mouth which tends to overshare at every possible opportunity would let others down. I thought that being Autistic, being from a working-class background, having a love of the arts and red lipstick, idiosyncratic humour, and an all-round eccentric personality would immediately disqualify someone like me from being the right type of person.

I was pleasantly surprised by the Nolan Principles as they consisted of:

- Selflessness

- Integrity

- Objectivity

- Accountability

- Openness

- Honesty

- Leadership.

These are all qualities that the majority of Autistic women and girls I know effortlessly possess. These principles, instead of the assumed rule book that ties someone down and removes their edge, actually give great freedom and make space for spiky, star-shaped individuality. As long as these principles are at the heart of your everyday code of conduct, all other eccentricity, disability, diversity and lifestyles are acceptable.

What if more employers, companies and organizations could accept Autistic women in this way? A rule book that doesn't give demands, such as: "You must wear a grey suit, cut your hair into a sensible style whilst having elocution classes and for God sake woman don't wear that animal print coat with red lipstick – it does nothing to hide the fact you only got an advocacy platform by winning sexiest woman of the year in your late twenties" but instead provides a framework that allows for individuality and acceptance, and embraces social mobility, eccentricity, neurodivergency and Autism. A workplace where you don't need to mask to fit in.

In an ideal world, companies, organizations and boards would be proactive and headhunt using a free to sign up for database of disabled applicants who would like to apply for a job within that organization. The very same day the advert for a vacancy goes on their website so would accessible application information and forms, if the website is not already universally accessible. We are not there yet!

Equal access to safeguarding in health care

Waking up from my emergency appendectomy late one night in 1996, in the new teen ward of the local hospital, I tried to sit up. Naively unaware of the recovery time needed and the seriousness and pain abdominal surgery brings, I vomited and almost passed out. Even with a super high pain threshold, golly that hurt. The nurse on duty was incredible. She cleaned me up and allowed me to sip water through what looked like a plastic lolly pop with sponge on the end (highly recommended sensory experience-wise if any fellow Autistics are reading!).

The nurse kindly took the alarm button off the wall behind me and placed it on the bedside cabinet and told me to just press it if I felt unwell again. She then went off to see the children in the children's ward, and with that I conceded my attempt to spring back to action, admitted pain threshold defeat and laid down to rest in the silence of the teen ward where I was the only resident that night.

Sometime later, I woke to find a man who must have been at least 30 sitting on the end of my hospital bed. He wasn't in uniform, which I thought was odd, so I assumed he must have been going home for the day.

"What are you in here for?" he asked.

"I had to have my appendix removed" I said, wondering why he didn't already know.

"Are you a doctor?" I asked.

"No, my daughter's only six and she's in the children's ward next door, she's having her appendix out too!"

"Oh, wow, really? I'm sorry."

"I'm really scared. I'm worried about her scar...show me your scar so I know what it looks like?" he almost demanded.

"I can't show you it, I'm not decent I only have my hospital gown on, sorry." I felt awful that I couldn't help, there was a scared dad worried about his daughter who was less than half my age, I decided to not show him how much pain I was in as I didn't want him to feel worse.

"Don't worry about that, just show me!" I thought he was getting more annoyed at me now or maybe just more scared about his daughter.

"I'm so sorry, I can't even sit upright now", I said, smiling with the fake brave face smile.

"Can you walk?" he asked.

I honestly shook my head, no.

"Can you run? If you really needed to?"

By this point I felt a strange feeling in my gut, in hindsight it was probably fear but I assumed it was because I was going to be sick again. Remembering the kind nurse's rule to "press this button if you feel unwell again" I tried to reach for the bedside cabinet but even stretching my right hand it felt like my stomach was ripping from the inside out. It probably was.

Luckily, and only by luck, the kind nurse appeared through the glass door that separated the teen ward to the children's ward. She was slim and not very tall but somehow had the strength to drag this dad away from the end of the bed and yell for security all at once.

"Please don't be cross with him!" I begged, "He is just scared about his daughter having her appendix out too."

The nurse's face went strange. In hindsight I think it was fury. He didn't have a daughter in the next ward. I know that now because the nurse told me afterwards that I was the only person who had an appendix removal and that there was no six-year-old girl in the children's ward that night. I still don't know who he was or why he was sitting on the end of my bed. I still don't know why the red flags of him not being in uniform didn't make me reach for the alarm buzzer sooner.

I do know, however, the importance of tweaking safeguarding instructions for Autistic girls in hospital.

I was the lucky one; I was only there a few nights. As an adult looking back, I worry for Autistic girls in mental health wards for months. What about the Autistic girls in residential care homes for years? What can be tweaked to ensure Autistic girls' safety in healthcare settings?

I was, of course, having the emergency surgery as I wasn't aware how much pain I was in fast enough. I'll take you back to the morning of that event. It's a long story but the context within it can and does help others each time I share it at conferences, so I'd like to share it here too.

I'd woken up with what I wasn't sure was either a headache or a stomach ache. As I was at that point a "serial school bunker", or in today's more kind terms "school refusing", it's fair to say that my parents were pretty fed up with me faking being unwell to get a day off. They had every reason to believe I was faking it as, in their defence, nine times out of ten, I was – I detested school. Unfortunately for me, this time I wasn't faking it. Think boy who cried wolf here!

I took it upon myself to go to the GP alone and he inspected my stomach. "Ah, you have appendicitis!" he said, fairly astonished I had not only managed to walk there but was smiling and cracking jokes on the doctor's couch. I tend to make jokes when I'm anxious. I also make jokes as a way to soundboard communication.

He printed off what looked like an A4 sized prescription on some pastel colour paper and said "As soon as you get home give this to your parents and go to hospital. You need surgery, I'm afraid." Of course, that wasn't my routine and, in my mind, "as soon as I get home" would be 4:30pm, about 6 hours from now. So, I took myself to school, on a bus, on the completely opposite side of town.

I was already late and feeling quite cold (in hindsight that was a fever) so I didn't go home to get my blazer and wore my prized possession of a Nike hoodie to school instead. For those who were raised in Bracknell in the 90s you'll understand why this was my prized possession – along with my gold sovereign ring, naturally.

At lunch I was hiding in the canteen hall as I didn't have my blazer on which was a weird rule of that particular school (and I was in a position to compare as I'd been ejected from other schools). "Why don't you have your blazer on, Carly Jones?" I had been spotted by a teacher. Sitting there, hood up and face flat on the canteen table to avoid eye contact, I replied, "Got appendicitis, Sir".

"No, you haven't if you had appendicitis you'd be in enormous pain and seriously unwell and you're clearly not!" I was kicked out of canteen with no lunch, which for 14-year-old me was more than a good enough reason to jump the school gate and go home.

My parents are phenomenally hard-working people so it wasn't until much later in the day that I was able to give them the now-crumpled bit of pastel paper the doctor had given me hours ago. I can't imagine what went through my poor folks' minds at the point of reading it, but I do remember my dad driving with some haste to the hospital.

Dad always has a way of making a serious situation more bearable with his dark but honest humour, "Don't worry, Carly, my appendix burst open before I knew I had it!" he disclosed. And people ask me who I take after?

As an adult and an Autism advocate, I am fascinated to hear the same tale time and time again of Autistic adults having experienced an emergency appendectomy as children or teenagers. But why?

Autistic people of all ages and genders have different sensory profiles. We can be hypo (under) sensitive or hyper (over) sensitive to:

- taste

- touch

- smell

- sight

- sounds.

We have additional senses, including:

- Vestibular

  - The vestibular system is our balance and movement sense.

  - It tells us where our body is in relation to gravity, where it is moving and how fast.

- Proprioception

  - This is our sense of body awareness.

  - Messages from muscles provide information about where our body is in space, and how it is moving (direction, speed and force) without using vision.

  - It is proprioception that allows us to move our hands carefully without having to observe every movement.

And the much less spoken about but vastly important…

- Interoception

  - Intereoception is a sensation related to the physiological/physical condition of the body, processing sensations inside of us. For some this may be finding it difficult to know when we are thirsty or when we have drunk too much. Knowing when we are hungry and need to eat, or knowing when we are full and to stop eating. Differences with interoception can affect an Autistic girl knowing she is pregnant, if she is in pain, if she needs the toilet, and yes, if her appendix is just about to burst.

There is a super important factor to remember here:

Just as Autistic girls can have a serious illness (appendicitis) and be none the wiser or have had surgery one day and head back to school the next without painkillers, they may also be hypersensitive to other types of pain. For example, if my eyebrows are plucked with tweezers or I have to wear a top with a label in, I'm in pain. It's quite difficult for professionals to understand how a patient who couldn't cope with a plaster being removed is later in need of serious help, but is sitting there making jokes and looking fine.

Just because an Autistic girl is hypersensitive to some pain, she most definitely can be hyposensitive to other types of pain – particularly when it's interoceptive (happening inside us).

I'm going to be really frank now: with this in mind, it's no surprise that the life expectancy for Autistic people is so much lower. Researchers from Sweden's Karolinska Institute found that the average age of death for Autistic people is just 58 years of age.[40] Even more worrying were the findings that Autistic people with learning disabilities had an average life expectancy of just 39.5 years of age.

Autistic people have spiky profiles intellectually, so who's to say who has a learning disability and who doesn't? In my area of ability, I have a very high IQ. Conversely, if you watch me buy something when you have to type in numbers to order, you'll see that whatever arrives down the conveyor belt is just as much a surprise to me as it is to you. It would be fair to say that our Autistic profiles are a blend of areas of great learning ability and learning disability.

Leading causes of death included epilepsy, which many Autistic people have as well as being Autistic. Suicide was another leading factor. Autistic people are nine times more likely to die by suicide than non-Autistic people. For non-Autistic people, men are 3.5 times more likely to die by suicide than non-Autistic women. Autistic women are more likely to die by suicide than non-Autistic men.

In 2016, I conducted a survey around the accessibility of crisis helplines following the tragedy of a young Autism advocate who sadly lost his life at a train station that year. The survey was called "Supporting Autistic People Using Helplines" and showed that 78 per cent of Autistic people asked felt they were unable to use a phone to make a call in a time of crisis.

Let's think about the other physical health factors though. How on earth can we have equal access to healthcare when nobody (sometimes not even us!) knows the seriousness of our pain, and can identify this in a timely way? Recognition of Autistic people's pain is vital because reporting pain and asking for help is much harder for us. Harder to recognize we are in pain because when everyday sensory input such as sounds, lights and fabrics cause great pain, what is an Autistic person's perception of being in no pain at all compared to a non-Autistic person? Do Autistic people have a higher baseline of pain? It's harder to report our pain too, as when we go over our particular pain threshold, many Autistic people who are quite verbal in their everyday life will become nonverbal.

In the first coronavirus lockdown, I was very concerned about the Autistic people I support and how they would be able to communicate their pain to their parents, carers, residential home staff, doctors, teachers etc. I designed and launched an app called "Visual Pain Images UK". Don't worry I'm not advertising to you here, it's completely free to use and I don't earn a penny from it in any capacity.

Visual Pain Images UK is, as it says on the tin, an app with images of what pain may "look" like. This isn't a new phenomenon and certainly not a genius innovation. People have used paper cutouts of body shapes so others can point to where it hurts for donkey's years.

The slight difference is, first, we may not always have our printed cutouts with us in an emergency, but we will almost always have our phones, tablets and smart watches. Even better, so do our doctors! Also, printed cutouts aren't as hygienic in a global pandemic and to know "where it hurts" first of all you have to know it actually hurts. If you don't know the sensation you're experiencing could be pain, you can't begin to point to where pain is. That's why technology, however well intended, should always be designed for the community it aims to serve; it misses the loopholes otherwise.

So, the images on the app include, for example, a photo of a balloon bulging as it's been tied up by an elastic band. This could give a visual prompt to describe bloating. A lightning flash could be used to prompt and communicate nerve pain. There is also a statement that a patient refuses a DNR (Do Not Resuscitate) order, which is terribly important at all times but particularly during the Covid pandemic when the boundary line between frailty scores and those with disabilities has been blurred.

Of course, the heart-wrenching and difficult lifesaving choices our doctors have to make can never be known, but my role as an advocate is to help give a voice to those unable to advocate for themselves and everyone deserves to have their wishes noted and heard, regardless of the outcome of those wishes.

The app is not Autism specific. As with anything I work on my hope is that, although it starts with an aim to safeguard a very specific community, it can work outwards and help other disabilities and conditions, or even simply be used because someone is abroad and can't speak the language or is alone and has a mouth injury. But the root of it all lies, of course, with the Autistic girls I support who are either nonverbal or have nonverbal periods. Not all Autistic people who talk are able to talk all the time.

I don't want to use up all your time and the entire book's word count on various accounts of my life story as it feels self-indulgent. We would be here for weeks and I don't want to bore you to tears.

Please just know that this going nonverbal business happens even in our late 30s, normally leaving healthcare teams and paramedics quite confused. There is a big contrast between the moment they first attended the scene and met someone who they assume is a permanently nonverbal Autistic woman, and the point five hours later when the pain management has kicked in and they find their "nonverbal" patient thanking them all and talking with great excitement and depth about Autism healthcare and the NHS in general.

Vaccines

What about Autistic girls' access to vaccines? Vaccines are often dished out via the mainstream school system. We already know that many Autistic girls are not in the mainstream school system but are instead home educated or receive education otherwise. How can they be protected with timely vaccines? Particularly the HPV vaccine which protects girls from cervical cancer later in life?

In 2019, I received a rather stark wake-up call via a letter telling me I had "High Grade, Severe Dyskaryosis", severe pre-cancer cells that need surgery to be removed – sharpish. Despite the panic, it got me doing better research than the FBI on cervical screening, abnormal cells and early cervical cancer data. What I learned from this hyperfocus created by the unwelcome arrival of dodgy cells was that there is a higher risk of abnormal cervical cells if a woman:

- doesn't have regular smear tests

- had sexual intercourse at an early age

- gave birth before the age of 17

- has had multiple partners

- has had HPV.

Have a look at this statistic:

- 19–31% of disabled women access smear tests as opposed to 73% of the general population.[41]

Autistic girls are often offered a tweaked (infantilized) sex education. But we must never assume that Autistic girls do not have sex lives.

Cancers

During a consultation meeting for the NHS, I got talking with an NHS cancer nurse. She told me that, in her experience, when she cares for Autistic cancer patients, they often come in at stage 3 or 4, not at stage 1 or 2. I spoke about Autism and interoception and how that can affect all Autistic people, with or without learning disabilities. She was as concerned as I am currently: bar a pilot in one area, Autistic people are only offered annual health checks if they also have a learning disability. This would be a bit like only offering glaucoma eye tests for those who need to wear glasses all the time as opposed to only for reading – it's illogical.

Explicit medication instructions

If you take instructions at face value or written words literally and are put on strong medication that states "take three times a day with food", what does that mean to you?

a. I eat three meals a day and will take one tablet with each meal.

b. I eat 10 times a day and will take three with each meal.

c. I only eat dinner; I don't like to eat lunch or breakfast, so I'll take three at once in the evening.

d. I have an eating disorder, I live off food replacement shakes and can't eat solid food – I won't take these.

You can see the importance of making sure instructions have been clearly understood.

STRATEGIES AND TIPS

-   Always offer explicit instructions on when an alarm button should be pressed. Perhaps "Please press this button should anyone not in uniform approach you [with visuals of all the staff on duty that shift], if you feel unwell or at any point want someone with you" could be a good safeguarding strategy. All staff would need to be trained to know this is the protocol.

- Autistic girls out of mainstream school should be alerted by the local authorities' home education team when their vaccines are due, and the local immunization team should chase these appointments up.

- All helplines need to have the funding, facility, training and staff to be able to offer text or email support rather than just phone calls.

- Doctors and pharmacies need to explain medication and give explicit instructions on when to take the medication that may be bespoke to each patient's lifestyle. It is vital that medical professionals take the concerns of parents, carers and Autistic people themselves incredibly seriously if a medication has had side effects previously to prevent harm or death.

Access to justice and legislative loopholes

Vicky was home alone when the police arrived at her address. The neighbours thought she may be self-harming a lot as they heard her vocalize and scream and one day the neighbours had got so concerned, they called the police. They were not aware Vicky was Autistic. She was in distress and unable to communicate so she reached into her pocket to grab a credit card sized awareness card that explains she is Autistic to others when she cannot talk.

As she reached into her pocket, the police officers, worried she had a weapon, such as a gun or more likely a knife, as self-harm had been reported, asked her to put her hands in the air. Vicky didn't; she wanted them to know she was Autistic so kept searching in her pocket for her alert card. Vicky was warned to put her hands in the air again, but as she refused, she was tasered.

I couldn't help but think of the consequences Vicky would have faced had she have been American and not British. Would she have been shot dead instead of tasered? What about the Autistic girls in other countries with varying gun laws and police procedures?

In 2017, I worked with a charity and one of the UK's largest police forces, hoping to open up a discourse around Autistic adults in police custody and in legal proceedings either as a witness, defendant or victim. I wanted the Autistic community to feel able to give feedback in an anonymous manner so again relied on the use of an informal survey to gain insights wider than my own perspectives.[42]

Fifty Autistic adults replied from around the world, not just the UK.

- 74% felt that Autistic adults had no access to a fair trial with unequal experiences in the legal system.

- 37% said it would take them longer than non-Autistic people to report a crime against them.

- "When I reported a crime, I was asked, 'Have I had sex before?' I said no. [She responds later on] Why did I say No? She didn't mention that it was the rape she was referring to, in which case, of course, it's rape, not sex." (Anon survey respondent)

- 100% felt that, as an Autistic adult in custody being overwhelmed with questioning, they would be vulnerable to making a false confession to make the questioning end.

- "Police need to stop making assumptions based on attitude, appearance etc. They judge books by their covers and write people off. I can see why they do this – they are busy and have learned a 'shorthand' way of categorising people into threatening/non-threatening, trustworthy/untrustworthy." (Anon survey respondent)

The theme of the United Nations Sustainable Developmental Goals "No one left behind" must be in the mindset of all policies. This doesn't need to be specific to Autistic girls or even disability focused, it just needs to find the hardest to reach and most vulnerable and overlooked in society then work from that position outwards. Autistic girls are therefore a sensible place to start because when we reach the hardest to reach, we reach everyone else along the way.

STRATEGIES AND TIPS

- There should be mandatory Autism training for all legal professionals, be that police, judges, lawyers, and especially court intermediaries.

- More than Easy Read is needed in court proceedings. We need Autism trained Court intermediaries who know how to translate implicit questions into context filled explicit questions.

- Let's think again about the Autistic mum in child custody proceedings asked, "So you've been on a parenting course, what was the best thing you got out of it?" (Implicit question)

   She replied, "I met another Autistic mum. I don't feel alone anymore, we are meeting up on Friday." That was noted as "mum has no concept of child's needs before own".

   Had they asked, "So you've been in a parenting

course, what was the best parenting strategy you learned?" she would have answered differently as this question had context and was explicit.

She lost her son.

- Outdated laws and new policies should be examined and drafted through an Autistic filter, by Autistic professionals, academics and policy makers with a view to protect the most vulnerable.

Child marriage

In England, you can currently marry at the age of 16, with your parent's consent. As discussed in Chapter 2, I strongly believe the legal age of marriage in the UK must be raised; it is a disability issue as much as a cultural one.

I've heard of Autistic girls being thrown out of cars as they are expecting an unplanned pregnancy out of marriage. I cannot see how marriage is safe for any 16 year old, let alone a disabled child.

As an Autistic woman married in my teens, this could be biased. I hope it's not. I still very much believe in marriage and would like to marry again when the time is right. Marriage isn't just about a white dress and a cake, however, it's a binding life long legal contract which affects your personal freedoms, finances and that of your children until death unless you are able to get out of it with support. What if the spouse you are hoping to divorce from is the only support you have? Divorce even at its most amicable is costly, exhausting and loaded with unexpected emotions; divorce at its most toxic causes many people life long devastation. It is not a future hurdle we should put up for a disabled child who's even less likely to have the support to escape the binds, not part of how the UK, or any country, should be safeguarding our most vulnerable.

Financial abuse[43]

How can we protect victims of economic abuse in a paperless financial world?

A few years ago, travelling home from a role in New York. I shared a flight with a gentleman who works in financial technology (fintech). As he spoke about the positives of online loans, I asked how any company could be sure any loan was not fraudulent? How does he prove someone's identity before giving the paperless loan the green light? He explained the checks consisted of photo ID, often a photo driving licence. So, I asked what happens in the case of economic abuse. How can a paperless loan provider be sure that the applicant ID has a valid and up-to-date address?

Many victims of economic abuse only discover their address has been used to take out loans when they receive related mail, so with paperless loans and even mortgages becoming more commonplace how would victims find out?

I had a good reason to look for answers on this topic like an over-talkative, world's worst spontaneous flight buddy. In my role, I support some of the UK's most vulnerable women; many are victims of economic abuse. One common experience is the use of a victim's address for years after they have separated from their partner.

Take, for example, the photo driving licence, commonly regarded as evidence of residence for paperless online loans. If the address is fake the only person who can remove the address is the licence holder themselves, not the DVLA or the homeowner whose address they have used fraudulently. I'm not talking about someone who lived at the same address but forgot to update their details. I'm talking about former partners who have deliberately applied for loans using the once shared address, months and years after not living together.

The DVLA, once it has been contacted by the victim of economic abuse, can stop an address being used again in the future, but only when the perpetrator applies for their next renewal. Driving licences usually need to be renewed every ten years.

Yes, you read that right, every TEN years.

So, what happens in that ten-year period in a fast paced, financial, paperless world where driving licences are accepted as proof of residence? Financial technology is the future, but with this must come modern tighter regulations, and robust policies to limit chances of fraudulent address use, and ultimately protect victims of economic abuse.

Care or control? Legal loopholes

Domestic violence, in all its forms, is taken extremely seriously in the UK. In 2015, Theresa May, the then Home Secretary, introduced legislation to make coercive control a criminal act recognized by the courts in England and Wales. This move was reflected also in Scotland, where the Domestic Abuse Bill that was passed in 2018 created a specific offence of "abusive behaviour in relation to a partner or ex-partner. This includes psychological abuse such as coercive and controlling behaviour as well as violence". Disabled women and Autistic women, like all women, are protected by this legislation.

There is, however, a potential loophole or grey area of defence criteria that could be misused against disabled/Autistic women due to the abuser being legally able to declare responsibility for their victim. In this context, there is the potential for the woman in such cases to be unprotected by this legislation.

Similarly, in England, one has to still be in a personal relationship with their abuser in order to be fully protected by the coercive control legislation. (In Scotland the wording includes "ex-partner".) It is a sad fact that many ex-spouses and partners who have acted in a coercive manner will use the family court system to hold reign over their ex-partners for years, possibly decades, after an intimate relationship has ended.

We must have user-led draft, review and editing processes

for all policies, guidelines and laws to be able to safeguard. This will help us to consign the grey areas to the shredder like in the apprentice NVQ days, and watertight the future safety of Autistic girls reaching all by proxy on the way, stopping these decades long patterns and systematic flow charts of vulnerability, forever.

Final Words

Finding someone who speaks your language is a beautiful and rare thing as an Autistic female.

Autism is often described as a spectrum. For me it often feels like a frequency; living a life with a somewhat different (not broken just different!) car radio that is often full of confusing static, half-understood words, perhaps interrupted by pirate stations or airline communication feedback, overlapping sounds that often give more confusion than pleasure. You can choose to switch your radio off forever or choose to continue scrolling the airwaves.

Now and then, you'll scroll through the available frequencies and at last you'll find a clear signal.

Some days it could be the news station and you are happy, educated and fulfilled for a while – just gratefully relieved from the unbearable static – but you were looking for something more upbeat, so you keep scrolling again through the static, distress and confusion. Eventually you come across a classical music station, you feel serene and comforted, but it's not your favourite music genre, so you boldly go for it again and start scrolling.

One day you'll be driving along an unknown road when quite by accident through the distraction static, you'll tune into a crystal-clear frequency playing a long forgotten, favourite song you adored. You forgot how that song made you feel and everything about your day and life seems, for that moment at least, perfectly on time, in sync, long awaited, happy, energized and, finally, safe.

Sometimes we can only keep transmitting our own frequency as loud as possible in the hope others pick up our signal.

Advocacy is how I try to do that.

There's a frequency for everyone out there flying through the airwaves if we blast ours out consistently enough.

Non-Autistic readers, please try one strategy from this book, and thank you for taking the time to tune in.

Autistic readers, thank you for being the reason to write this book. Never forget to keep scrolling the bloody radio, keep defying gravity.

Endnotes

1   Jones, C. (2015) 'The importance of a timely Autism diagnosis to prevent the Autistic community from abuse.' Survey monkey informal community survey.

2   Hirvikoski, T., Mittendorfer-Rutz, E., Boman, M., Larsson, H., Lichtenstein, P. & Bölte, S. (2016) 'Premature mortality in autism spectrum disorder.' *British Journal of Psychiatry 208*, 3, 232–238. Accessed on 05 May 2021 at https://pubmed.ncbi.nlm.nih.gov/26541693.

3   www.cornwallvsf.org/wp-content/uploads/2018/07/Autism-diagnosis-crisis-FOI-response-briefing.pdf.

4   National Autistic Society (NAS) (n.d.) 'Diagnostic tools – a guide for all audiences.' Accessed on 05 May 2021 at www.autism.org.uk/advice-and-guidance/topics/diagnosis/diagnostic-tools/all-audiences.

5   www.who.int/classifications/icd/en/bluebook.pdf.

6   www.thedsm5.com/the-dsm-5.

7   www.autism.org.uk/advice-and-guidance/topics/diagnosis/diagnostic-tools.

8   Autism Research Centre, University of Cambridge (2021) 'Empathy Quotient for adults.' Accessed on 05 May 2021 at www.autismresearchcentre.com/tests/empathy-quotient-eq-for-adults.

9   Autism Research Centre, University of Cambridge (2021) 'Autism Spectrum Quotient for adults.' Accessed on 05 May 2021 at www.autismresearchcentre.com/tests/autism-spectrum-quotient-aq-adult.

10 www.nhs.uk/conditions/bipolar-disorder/symptoms.

11 www.nhs.uk/conditions/borderline-personality-disorder.

12 www.nhs.uk/conditions/dissociative-disorders.

13 Jones, C., Moyse, R. & Evans, M. (2017) 'Written evidence from British autism advocates.' CHM00026. [Submitted to UK Parliament Health Committee for Children and Young People] Accessed on 20 May 2021 at https://old.parliament.uk/business/committees/committees-a-z/commons-select/health-committee/inquiries/parliament-2015/children-young-people-mental-health-education-inquiry-16-17/publications/?fbclid=IwAR03xPgbA6ZuLKhkSdaAACDpGti-FQHZfPEhPVy9dCxHpgLd6EwMdtfıK5M.

14 Jones, C. (2016) 'Hidden cost of a late Autism diagnosis.' Survey monkey informal community survey.

15 Jones, C. (2015) 'The importance of a timely Autism diagnosis to prevent the Autistic community from abuse.' Survey monkey informal community survey.

16 Safeguarding Course within VPI UK app. See www.google.co.uk/amp/s/appadvice.com/app/visual-pain-images-vpi-uk/1533799859.amp.

17 Safeguarding Course within VPI UK app. See www.google.co.uk/amp/s/appadvice.com/app/visual-pain-images-vpi-uk/1533799859.amp.

18 Jones, C. (2015) 'The importance of a timely Autism diagnosis to prevent the Autistic community from abuse.' Survey monkey informal community survey.

19 Davison, S. (2018) 'Does ABA harm autistic people?' Accessed on 20 May 2021 at https://autisticuk.org/does-aba-harm-autistic-people.

20 https://home/chronos/u-7111221a93fc90486cc578edb1d1e02be27ecc61/MyFiles/Downloads/WulffASDHIV1%20(2).pdf.

21 Hill, A. (2016) 'Autism: "Hidden pool" of undiagnosed mothers with condition emerging. *The Guardian*, 26 December. Accessed on 05 May 2021 at www. theguardian.com/society/2016/dec/26/autism-hidden-pool-of-undiagnosed-mothers-with-condition-emerging.

22 Donovan, J. (2020) 'Childbirth experiences of women with Autism Spectrum Disorder in an acute care setting.' *Nursing for Women's Health 24*, 3, 165–174. Accessed on 05 May 2021 at www.sciencedirect.com/science/article/abs/pii/S1751485120300684.

23 National Autistic Society/Department for Education (2019) 'Safeguarding young people on the Autism Spectrum.' Accessed on 05 May 2021 at https://preventforfeandtraining.org.uk/wp-content/uploads/2019/07/NAS_SafeguardingYoungPeople.pdf.

24 www.smallpeicetrust.org.uk/cyberfirst.

25 https://preventforfeandtraining.org.uk/wp-content/uploads/2019/07/NAS_SafeguardingYoungPeople.pdf.

26 Oxford City Council (2021). 'Cuckooing.' Accessed on 05 May 2021 at www.oxford.gov.uk/info/20101/community_safety/1308/cuckooing.

27 See www.nottingham.ac.uk/psychology/people/sarah.cassidy.

28 www.whatsthedebate.co.uk.

29 The MASH is a team of co-located multi agency safeguarding partners, who research, interpret and determine appropriate information sharing in relation to children, young people (and vulnerable adults) at risk of immediate and / or serious harm. It receives child welfare referrals via the integrated Early Help and Social Work Triage. See https://rotherhamscb.proceduresonline.com/chapters/p_action_follow.html#:~:text=The%20MASH%20is%20a%20team,at%20risk%20of%20immediate%20and%20%2F.

30 https://carolgraysocialstories.com.

31 Shah, A. (2019) *Catatonia, Shutdown and Breakdown in Autism: A Psycho-Ecological Approach*. London: Jessica Kingsley Publishers.

32   Adewunmi, B. (2014) 'Kimberle Crenshaw on intersectionality: "I wanted to come up with an everyday metaphor that anyone could use".' *New Statesman*. Accessed on 03 August 2021 at https://www.newstatesman. com/lifestyle/2014/04/kimberl-crenshaw-intersectionality-i-wanted-come-everyday-metaphor-anyone-could.

33   Deweerdt, S. (2020) 'Eyeing the connection between autism and vision.' *Spectrum*. Accessed on 03 August 2021 at https://www.spectrumnews.org/ features/deep-dive/eyeing-the-connection-between-autism-and-vision/ amp.

34   National Autistic Society (n.d.) 'Autistic women and girls.' Accessed on 05 May 2021 at www.autism.org.uk/advice-and-guidance/what-is-autism/ autistic-women-and-girls.

35   Edwards, O. & Jones, C. (2015) 'Gender fluidity prism in diagnosis of autism.' *International Journal of Sciences: Basic and Applied Research (IJS-BAR) 24*, 4, 163–169. Accessed on 05 May 2021 at https://peacefestival.us/ wp-content/uploads/2015/11/Olley-Edwards.pdf.

36   Jones, C. (2015) 'Autism and BAME women.' Survey monkey informal community survey.

37   Pohl, A.L., Crockford, S.K., Blakemore, M., Allison, C. & Baron-Cohen, S. (2020) 'A comparative study of autistic and non-autistic women's experience of motherhood.' *Molecular Autism 11*, 3. Accessed on 05 May 2021 at https://molecularautism.biomedcentral.com/articles/10.1186/ s13229-019-0304-2.

38   www.ons.gov.uk/peoplepopulationandcommunity/healthandsocialcare/ disability/articles/outcomesfordisabledpeopleintheuk/2020.

39   https://www.learningdisabilities.org.uk/learning-disabilities/a-to-z/e/ easy-read#:~:text=%20There%20are%20various%20different%20 ways%20in%20which,as%20A5%20or%20smaller%20are%20not...%20 More%20.

40   Hirvikoski, T., Mittendorfer-Rutz, E., Boman, M., Larsson, H., Lichtenstein, P. & Bölte, S. (2016) 'Premature mortality in autism spectrum disorder.' *British Journal of Psychiatry 208*, 3, 232–238. Accessed on 05 May 2021 at https://pubmed.ncbi.nlm.nih.gov/26541693.

41   Thornton, J. (2019) 'People with learning disabilities have lower life expectancy and cancer screening rates.' *British Medical Journal*. Accessed on 05 May 2021 at www.bmj.com/content/364/bmj.l404.

42   Jones, C. (2017) 'Global stats on Autism and police.' Informal community survey.

43   www.ons.gov.uk/peoplepopulationandcommunity/healthandsocialcare/ disability/articles/outcomesfordisabledpeopleintheuk/2020.

Useful Resources and Recommended Reading

There are many brilliant resources for and about Autistic girls, both the older tried and tested and the new, innovative and inspiringly ground-breaking. There is a huge risk in only recommending a select few that I may neglect to remember to add more and kick myself later on post print. If I have done so, please forgive me!

This list is by no means exhaustive, but it's a starting point.

Books

Bargiela, S. (2019) *Camouflage: The Hidden Lives of Austisic Women.* London: Jessica Kingsley Publishers.

Beardon, L. (2010) *Autism in Adults.* London: Sheldon Press.

Cook, B. and Garnett, M. (eds) (2018) *Spectrum Women: Walking to the Beat of Autism.* London: Jessica Kingsley Publishers.

Ekins, E. (2021) *Queerly Autistic: The Ultimate Guide for LGBT-QIA+ Teens on the Spectrum.* London: Jessica Kingsley Publishers.

Hendrickx, S. and Gould, J. (2015) *Women and Girls with Autism Spectrum Disorder: Understanding Life Experiences from Early Childhood to Old Age.* London: Jessica Kingsley Publishers.

Holliday Willey, L. (2014) *Pretending to Be Normal.* London: Jessica Kingsley Publishers.

James, L. (2017) *Odd Girl Out: An Autistic Woman in a Neurotypical World.* London: Bluebird.

Lucas, R. (2017) *The State of Grace.* London: Macmillan.

Moyse, R. (2020) 'Missing: The autistic girls absent from mainstream secondary schools.' PhD thesis. University of Reading. Accessed on 18 May 2021 at http://centaur.reading.ac.uk/97405.

Quinn, A. (2018) *Unbroken: Learning to Live Beyond Diagnosis.* Newark: Trigger Publishing.

Shah, A. (2019) *Catatonia, Shutdown and Breakdown in Autism: A Psycho-Ecological Approach.* London: Jessica Kingsley Publishers.

Silberman, S. (2015) *Neurotribes.* New York: Allen and Unwin.

Simone, R. (2010) *Aspergirls: Empowering Females with Asperger's Syndrome.* London: Jessica Kingsley Publishers.

Students of Limpsfield Grange School and Martin, V. (2015) *M Is for Autism.* London: Jessica Kingsley Publishers.

Charities and Organizations

A2nd Voice

Autism Berkshire

Autism Pride Reading

Dogs for Autism

Include Me Too

National Autistic Society

Parenting Special Children

Websites

British Autism Advocate: https://britishautismadvoc.wixsite.com/carlyjonesmbe

The Equality Act (2010) UK: www.legislation.gov.uk/ukpga/2010/15/contents

Financial Abuse Code of Practice: www.ukfinance.org.uk/financial-abuse-code-practice. Many UK banks and buildings societies have signed up to this and abide by its phenomenal guidelines.

Purple Ella: https://www.purpleella.com

Scottish Women's Autism Network (SWAN): https://swanscotland.org

The Thinking Person's Guide to Autism: www.thinkingautismguide.com

What's the Debate cards: www.whatsthedebate.co.uk

Youtubers

Anna Moomin

Paige Layle

Chloe Hayden

Unfiltered Oversharing Acknowledgements

Lynda at JKP – thanks for inviting me to author this book, supporting me with the spelling and trusting me with such an important topic. I hope I haven't let you down. There's still time, the acknowledgements may lower the tone?

Dr Gould – thanks for the unofficial first day of the rest of my life and for so modestly changing the lives of Autistic girls throughout the globe – forever. I shudder to imagine what the world today would be like without you. You changed my life and countless others with such modesty and grace.

Mum and Dad – thank you for the official first day of my life and for making every day easier. You raised an Autistic girl in an age when Autistic girls pretty much didn't exist in the public and clinical world. God knows how. Thank you for everything, I'd be lost without you. Your work ethic and family loyalty I can only hope to live up to in my own responsibilities. I am forever in your debt (and if this book doesn't sell as well as I'd hope... that will be quite literally).

My girls – not enough words to thank you and praise you three for being the unique, kind, funny, resilient women you've become. Proud is probably the world's greatest understatement; I'm so lucky. I know you'll all do phenomenal things as the young women you are now and I'm excited for your futures.

Hunter the Wonder Dog – thank you for being the most loyal four-legged friend I've ever had (no offence any human friends, not that you have four legs) and helping C in the ways only you know how. The world's goodest boy.

Sharon – I could not have written this book without you. Not only the logistical dog care, but the hundreds of miles walking and talking in the last year. Here's to many more muddy woodland adventures where I fall on my arse in mud daily and you laugh in my face...daily.

Nan – thank you for teaching me selflessness, modest living, and family values.

Dr Beardon – for taking the time to read the first draft even though you were slammed with responsibilities and for always giving me a sense of self-confidence. And for the extraordinary geese photos.

Mel – for being the anytime of day or night friend and helping me kick imposter syndrome, and for being the true meaning of girl power, always raising women up and discreetly straightening even the most crooked of crowns. You are one in a million.

Julia and Wayne – for seeing my masking or indeed unmasking as a talent, never making me feel like a burden, assuring me I was in the room for talent not as a token and allowing me to try again and again until I could crack the nut. I could unmask with you as I felt safe with you, what a team.

Chris – for speaking the same language, making life make sense in the daily static and keeping me sane with your (terrible) but much appreciated puns. Alanis would be proud. Thanks for tolerating me.

Gay dad Brad – for being the best male friend an Autistic woman could ask for to help raise her girls. You're always there for us all when it matters: school plays, pick up time, birthdays, moving house, life's ups, life's lows, being a dodgy smear test LLETZ treatment hand-holder. Probably time to change my name from "I've seen inside of her" on your phone contacts though – bit embarrassing down the pub. Thanks for always being there, albeit normally dressed in sequins.

Sam – for still being my friend, often in the hardest scenarios, even after I dropped out of university almost 15 years ago and left you to do it on your own (you rock).

Rachel and Lorraine – for doing what you do and making accessibility and awareness for Autistic girls happen UK-wide (insert a troll with a party blower sound effect here).

Mairi – for being my official unofficial supervisor, confident Queen and kitten photo sender.

Ruth – for your years of belief and support and dedication to Autistic girls out of education.

Paula – for teaching me how to handle complaints with dignity and inspiring me with your super-human emotional strength.

Julie – for keeping our local girls safe and happy in art class, you're an earth Angel.

Catriona – for solidarity in a collective mission to safeguard Autistic girls, swimming like swans. Scotland's lucky to have you!

Dena – for holding my hand at the United Nations in 2014 and making me feel at home in NYC.

Louise – for embracing the value of both social mobility and neurodivergency in your team and always responding to my highly unprofessional anxiety-laced emails even if on a Saturday morning! The world needs more of you.

Index

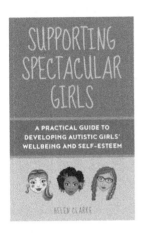

Supporting Spectacular Girls

A Practical Guide to Developing Autistic Girls' Wellbeing and Self-Esteem

Helen Clarke

£18.99 | $27.95 | PB | 288PP |
ISBN 978 1 78775 548 2 |
eISBN 978 1 78775 549 9

Autistic girls can be frequently misunderstood, underestimated and therefore anxious in a school environment. This practical book offers an innovative life skills curriculum for autistic girls aged 11 to 15, based on the author's successful workshops and training, which show how to support girls' wellbeing and boost their self-esteem.

Including an adapted PSHE curriculum, this is a straightforward guide to educating autistic children on the issues that matter most to them. It covers all essential areas of wellbeing, including communication, identity, self-regulation and triggers, safety, and physical and mental health, and offers the reader strategies to help the autistic girls in their lives enhance and develop these.

Helen Clarke worked as a teacher of autistic children for 20 years, and now runs her own autism consultancy (https://helenclarkeautism.com), providing autism training to schools and organizations. As an autistic woman herself, and with an autistic daughter, she is particularly passionate about supporting autistic girls to achieve good health and reach their academic potential. Helen is a public speaker and spoke at the recent NAS Women and Girls conference.

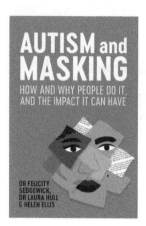

Autism and Masking

How and Why People Do It, and the Impact It Can Have

Dr Felicity Sedgewick,
Dr Laura Hull and Helen Ellis

£16.99 | $24.95 | PB | 272PP |
ISBN 978 1 78775 579 6 |
eISBN 978 1 78775 580 2

This book combines the latest research with personal case studies detailing autistic experiences of masking. It explains what masking is and the various strategies used to mask in social situations. The research also delves into the psychology behind masking and the specifics of masking at school, at social events with peers, and at work. The book looks at the consequences of masking, including the toll it can have on mental and physical health, and suggests guidance for family, professionals and employers to ameliorate negative effects.

Dr Felicity Sedgewick is a developmental and social psychologist, and lectures on Psychology of Education at the University of Bristol. Her research focuses on the social lives and mental health of autistic people of all genders, through a variety of research methods.

Dr Laura Hull is a post-doctoral researcher at University College London. Her research focuses on masking and camouflaging in autism, with a specific focus on how these impact diagnosis and mental health outcomes for autistic young people and adults.

Helen Ellis is an autistic adult who was diagnosed in her early 20s and has spent the past decade participating in various research studies and giving talks about being autistic. Her main areas of interest are employment, masking and burnout, wellbeing and special interests.

The **#ActuallyAutistic**
Guide to Advocacy

Step-by-Step Advice on How to
Ally and Speak UP with Autistic
People and the Autism Community

Jennifer Brunton, PhD and Jenna Gensic

£15.99 | $21.95 | PB | 320PP |
ISBN 978 1 78775 973 2 |
eISBN 978 1 78775 974 9

The #ActuallyAutistic Guide to Advocacy takes an in-depth look at the key elements of effective, respectful, inclusive advocacy and allyship. Every topic was chosen, shaped and informed by #ActuallyAutistic perspectives.

The step-by-step guide discusses various aspects of how autism is perceived, explores how best to speak up for individual needs, and introduces advocacy for the wider autistic community. Each step outlines one vital aspect of advocacy and allyship, such as emphasizing acceptance, avoiding assumptions and assuming competence. The advice and strategies laid out in this guide centre the wisdom and experiences of Autistic people and enable the reader to confidently speak up with insight and understanding.

Dr Jennifer Elizabeth Brunton is a neurodivergent academic turned freelance writer and editor. She is an academic with extensive writing and editing experience from a variety of diverse publications. She also runs the neurodiverse parenting and advocacy blog, Full Spectrum Mama.

Jenna Gensic is a freelance writer and disability advocate. Jenna is the author of *What Your Child on the Spectrum Really Needs: Advice From 12 Autistic Adults*, and she manages the Learn from Autistics website and regularly engages with the autistic community and shares autistic expertise. She has an autistic brother and son and writes and speaks about parenting issues related to prematurity, cerebral palsy and autism.